CAROLING DUSK

Books by Countee Cullen

Color
Copper Sun
The Ballad of the Brown Girl
The Medea
The Lost Zoo
My Lives and How I Lost Them
On These I Stand
One Way to Heaven

Edited by Countee Cullen

Caroling Dusk

CAROLING
DUSK

An Anthology of Verse
by Negro Poets

Edited by
COUNTEE CULLEN, 1903 – 1946, ed.

HARPER & ROW, PUBLISHERS
New York, Evanston, San Francisco, London

ACKNOWLEDGMENTS

For permission to use the poems in this anthology, the editor wishes to thank the poets represented, and the following magazines and publishers:

Dodd, Mead and Co. for poems from *The Collected Poems of Paul Laurence Dunbar*

Boni and Liveright for poems from *Cane* by Jean Toomer

Alfred A. Knopf for poems from *The Weary Blues* and *Fine Clothes to the Jew* by Langston Hughes

The Viking Press for "The Creation" from *God's Trombones* by James Weldon Johnson

The Cornhill Publishing Co. for poems from *The Band of Gideon* by Joseph S. Cotter, and from *Fifty Years and other Poems* by James Weldon Johnson, and from *The Heart of a Woman* by Georgia Douglas Johnson

Harcourt, Brace & Co. for poems from *Harlem Shadows* by Claude McKay and for *A Litany of Atlanta* by W. E. B. DuBois

Harper & Brothers for poems from *Color* and *Copper Sun* by Countee Cullen

B. J. Brimmer Co. for poems from *Bronze* by Georgia Douglas Johnson

Opportunity: A Journal of Negro Life for *Desolate* and *My House* by Claude McKay; *Old Black Men* by Georgia Douglas Johnson; *Summer Matures, Fulfillment, The Road* by Helene Johnson; *Portrait* by George Leonard Allen; *For the Candlelight* by Angelina Weld Grimké; *The Return, Golgotha Is a Mountain, The Day Breakers,* and *God Give to Men* by Arna Bontemps; *I Have a Rendezvous With Life* by Countee Cullen; *Lines Written at the Grave of Alexander Dumas* and *Hatred* by Gwendolyn B. Bennett; *Joy, Solace, Interim* by Clarissa Scott Delany; *Confession* by Donald Jeffrey Hayes; *On Seeing Two Brown Boys In a Catholic Church* and *To a Persistent Phantom* by Frank Horne; *Poem* by Blanche Taylor Dickinson; *The New Negro* by James Edward McCall; *The Tragedy of Pete* and *The Wayside Well* by Joseph S. Cotter, Sr.; *No Images* by Waring Cuney; *No'thboun'* by Lucy Ariel Williams; *Shadow* by Richard Bruce; *The Resurrection* by Jonathan H. Brooks; *Africa* and *Transformation* by Lewis Alexander

The Conning Tower of the New York World for *Noblesse Oblige* by Jessie Redmond Fauset

The Crisis for *That Hill* by Blanche Taylor Dickinson; *Nocturne at Bethesda* by Arna Bontemps; *Letters Found Near a Suicide* by Frank Horne; *Morning Light* by Mary Effie Lee Newsome; *Dunbar* by Anne Spencer

The Century for *My City* by James Weldon Johnson

Vanity Fair for *Bottled* by Helene Johnson

Palms for *A Tree Design* by Arna Bontemps; *Lines to a Nasturtium* by Anne Spencer; *Black Madonna* by Albert Rice; *Words! Words!* by Jessie Fauset; *Magula* by Helene Johnson; and *The Mask* by Clarissa Scott Delany

Fire for *Jungle Taste* by Edward S. Silvera; *Length of Moon* by Arna Bontemps; *The Death Bed* by Waring Cuney

The World Tomorrow for *A Black Man Talks of Reaping* by Arna Bontemps

The Survey for *Russian Cathedral* by Claude McKay

The Atlantic Monthly for *Nativity* and *The Serving Girl* by Gladys Casley Hayford

The Carolina Magazine for *The Dark Brother* by Lewis Alexander

FOREWORD

It is now five years since James Weldon Johnson edited with a brilliant essay on "The Negro's Creative Genius" *The Book of American Negro Poetry*, four years since the publication of Robert T. Kerlin's *Negro Poets and Their Poems*, and three years since from the Trinity College Press in Durham, North Carolina, came *An Anthology of Verse by American Negroes*, edited by Newman Ivey White and Walter Clinton Jackson. The student of verse by American Negro poets will find in these three anthologies comprehensive treatment of the work of Negro poets from Phyllis Wheatley, the first American Negro known to have composed verses, to writers of the present day. With Mr. Johnson's scholarly and painstaking survey, from both a historical and a critical standpoint, of the entire range of verse by American Negroes, and with Professor Kerlin's inclusions of excerpts from the work of most of those Negro poets whose poems were extant at the time of his compilation, there would be scant reason for the assembling and publication of another such collection were it not for the new voices that within the past three to five years have sung so significantly as to make imperative an anthology recording some snatches of their songs. To those intelligently familiar with what is popularly termed the renaissance in art and literature by Negroes, it will not be taken as a sentimentally risky observation to contend that the recent yearly contests conducted by Negro magazines, such as *Opportunity* and *The Crisis,* as well as a growing tendency on the part of white editors to give impartial consideration to the work of Negro writers, have awakened to a happy articulation many young Negro poets who had thitherto lisped only in isolated places in solitary numbers. It is primarily to give them a concerted hearing that this collection has been published. For most of these poets the publication of individual volumes of their poems is not an immediate issue. However, many of their poems during these four or five years of accentuated interest in the artistic development of the race have become familiar to a large and ever-widening circle of readers who, we feel, will welcome a volume marshaling what would otherwise remain for some time a miscellany of deeply appreciated but scattered verse.

The place of poetry in the cultural development of a race or people has always been one of importance; indeed, poets are prone, with many good reasons for their conceit, to hold their art the most important. Thus while essentially wishing to draw the public ear to the work of the younger Negro poets, there have been included with their poems those of modern Negro poets already established and acknowledged, by virtue of their seniority and published books, as worthy practitioners of their art. There were Negro poets before Paul Laurence Dunbar, but his uniquity as the first Negro to attain to and maintain a distinguished place among

American poets, a place fairly merited by the most
acceptable standards of criticism, makes him the pivotal
poet of this volume.

I have called this collection an anthology of verse by
Negro poets rather than an anthology of Negro verse,
since this latter designation would be more confusing
than accurate. Negro poetry, it seems to me, in the
sense that we speak of Russian, French, or Chinese
poetry, must emanate from some country other than
this in some language other than our own. Moreover,
the attempt to corral the outbursts of the ebony muse
into some definite mold to which all poetry by Negroes
will conform seems altogether futile and aside from the
facts. This country's Negro writers may here and
there turn some singular facet toward the literary sun,
but in the main, since theirs is also the heritage of the
English language, their work will not present any seri-
ous aberration from the poetic tendencies of their times.
The conservatives, the middlers, and the arch heretics
will be found among them as among the white poets; and
to say that the pulse beat of their verse shows generally
such a fever, or the symptoms of such an ague, will
prove on closer examination merely the moment's exag-
geration of a physician anxious to establish a new liter-
ary ailment. As heretical as it may sound, there is the
probability that Negro poets, dependent as they are on
the English language, may have more to gain from the
rich background of English and American poetry than
from any nebulous atavistic yearnings toward an Afri-
can inheritance. Some of the poets herein represented

will eventually find inclusion in any discriminatingly ordered anthology of American verse, and there will be no reason for giving such selections the needless distinction of a separate section marked Negro verse.

While I do not feel that the work of these writers conforms to anything that can be called the Negro school of poetry, neither do I feel that their work is varied to the point of being sensational; rather is theirs a variety within a uniformity that is trying to maintain the higher traditions of English verse. I trust the selections here presented bear out this contention. The poet writes out of his experience, whether it be personal or vicarious, and as these experiences differ among other poets, so do they differ among Negro poets; for the double obligation of being both Negro and American is not so unified as we are often led to believe. A survey of the work of Negro poets will show that the individual diversifying ego transcends the synthesizing hue. From the roots of varied experiences have flowered the dialect of Dunbar, the recent sermon poems of James Weldon Johnson, and some of Helene Johnson's more colloquial verses, which, differing essentially only in a few expressions peculiar to Negro slang, are worthy counterparts of verses done by John V. A. Weaver "in American." Attempt to hedge all these in with a name, and your imagination must deny the facts. Langston Hughes, poetizing the blues in his zeal to represent the Negro masses, and Sterling Brown, combining a similar interest in such poems as "Long Gone" and "The Odyssey of Big Boy" with a capacity for turning a neat sonnet according to the rules, represent differences as unique as those between Burns and Whitman. Jessie Fauset with Cornell University and training at the Sorbonne as her intellectual equipment surely justifies the very subjects and forms of her poems: "Touché," "La Vie C'est la Vie," "Noblesse Oblige," etc.; while Lewis Alexander, with no known degree from the University of Tokyo, is equally within the province of his creative prerogatives in composing Japanese *hokkus* and *tankas*. Although Anne Spencer lives in Lynchburg, Virginia, and in her biographical note recognizes the Negro as the great American taboo, I have seen but two poems by her which are even remotely concerned with this subject; rather does she write with a cool precision that calls forth comparison with Amy Lowell and the influence of a rock-bound seacoast. And Lula Lowe Weeden, the youngest poet in the volume, living in the same Southern city, is too young to realize that she is colored in an environment calculated to impress her daily with the knowledge of this pigmentary anomaly.

There are lights and shades of difference even in their methods of decrying race injustices, where these peculiar experiences of Negro life cannot be overlooked. Claude McKay is most exercised, rebellious, and vituperative to a degree that clouds his lyricism in many instances, but silhouettes most forcibly his high dudgeon; while neither Arna Bontemps, at all times cool, calm, and intensely religious, nor Georgia Douglas Johnson, in many instances bearing up bravely under comparison with Sara Teasdale, takes advantage of the numerous opportunities offered them for rhymed polemics.

If dialect is missed in this collection, it is enough to state that the day of dialect as far as Negro poets are concerned is in the decline. Added to the fact that these poets are out of contact with this fast-dying medium, certain sociological considerations and the natural limitations of dialect for poetic expression militate against its use even as a *tour de force.* In a day when artificiality is so vigorously condemned, the Negro poet would be foolish indeed to turn to dialect. The majority of present-day poems in dialect are the efforts of white poets.

This anthology, by no means offered as *the* anthology of verse by Negro poets, is but a prelude, we hope, to that fuller symphony which Negro poets will in time contribute to the national literature, and we shall be sadly disappointed if the next few years do not find this collection entirely outmoded.

· · · · · · ·

The biographical notices carried with these poems have been written by the poets themselves save in three cases (Dunbar's having been written by his wife, the younger Cotter's by his father, and Lula Weeden's by her mother), and if they do not reveal to a curious public all it might wish to know about the poets, they at least reveal all that the poets deem necessary and discreet for the public to know.

COUNTEE CULLEN.

CONTENTS

FOREWORD vii

PAUL LAURENCE DUNBAR
Ere Sleep Comes Down to Soothe the Weary Eyes . . . 2
Death Song 4
Life 5
After the Quarrel 5
Ships that Pass in the Night 7
We Wear the Mask 8
Sympathy 8
The Debt 9

JOSEPH S. COTTER, SR.
The Tragedy of Pete 11
The Way-side Well 15

JAMES WELDON JOHNSON
From the German of Uhland 17
The Glory of the Day Was in Her Face 18
The Creation 19
The White Witch 22
My City 25

WILLIAM EDWARD BURGHARDT DU BOIS
A Litany of Atlanta 26

WILLIAM STANLEY BRAITHWAITE
Scintilla 31
Rye Bread 31
October XXIX, 1795 32
Del Cascar 33

JAMES EDWARD MCCALL
The New Negro 34

ANGELINA WELD GRIMKÉ
Hushed by the Hands of Sleep 36
Greenness 36

The Eyes of My Regret 37
Grass Fingers 38
Surrender 38
The Ways o' Men 39
Tenebris 40
When the Green Lies Over the Earth 41
A Mona Lisa 42
Paradox 43
Your Hands 44
I Weep 45
For the Candle Light 45
Dusk 46
The Puppet Player 46
A Winter Twilight 46

ANNE SPENCER
Neighbors 47
I Have a Friend 47
Substitution 48
Questing 48
Life-long, Poor Browning 49
Dunbar 50
Innocence 51
Creed 51
Lines to a Nasturtium 52
At the Carnival 53

MARY EFFIE LEE NEWSOME
Morning Light 55
Pansy 56
Sassafras Tea 56
Sky Pictures 57
The Quilt 58
The Baker's Boy 58
Wild Roses 59
Quoits 59

JOHN FREDERICK MATHEUS
Requiem 61

FENTON JOHNSON
When I Die 62

Puck Goes to Court 63
The Marathon Runner 64

JESSIE FAUSET
Words! Words! 65
Touché 66
Noblesse Oblige 67
La Vie C'est la Vie 69
The Return 70
Rencontre 70
Fragment 70

ALICE DUNBAR NELSON
Snow in October . . . . - 71
Sonnet 72
I Sit and Sew 73

GEORGIA DOUGLAS JOHNSON
Service 75
Hope 75
The Suppliant 76
Little Son 76
Old Black Men 77
Lethe 77
Proving 77
I Want to Die While You Love Me 78
Recessional 79
My Little Dreams 79
What Need Have I for Memory? 80
When I Am Dead 80
The Dreams of the Dreamer 80
The Heart of a Woman 81

CLAUDE McKAY
America 83
Exhortation: Summer, 1919 84
Flame-heart 85
The Wild Goat 87
Russian Cathedral 87
Desolate 88
Absence 91
My House 92

JEAN TOOMER

    Reapers 94
    Evening Song 94
    Georgia Dusk 95
    Song of the Son 96
    Cotton Song 97
    Face 98
    November Cotton Flower 99

JOSEPH S. COTTER, JR.

    Rain Music 100
    Supplication 101
    An April Day 102
    The Deserter 102
    And What Shall You Say? 103
    The Band of Gideon 103

BLANCHE TAYLOR DICKINSON

    The Walls of Jericho 106
    Poem 107
    Revelation 107
    That Hill 109
    To an Icicle 110
    Four Walls 110

FRANK HORNE

    On Seeing Two Brown Boys in a Catholic Church . . . 112
    To a Persistent Phantom 113
    Letters Found Near a Suicide 114
    Nigger 120

LEWIS ALEXANDER

    Negro Woman 122
    Africa 123
    Transformation 124
    The Dark Brother 124
    Tanka I—VIII 125
    Japanese Hokku 127
    Day and Night 129

STERLING A. BROWN

    Odyssey of Big Boy 130

Maumee Ruth 133
Long Gone 134
To a Certain Lady, in Her Garden 136
Salutamus 138
Challenge 138
Return 139

CLARISSA SCOTT DELANY
Joy 140
Solace 141
Interim 142
The Mask 143

LANGSTON HUGHES
I, Too 145
Prayer 146
Song for a Dark Girl 147
Homesick Blues 147
Fantasy in Purple 148
Dream Variation 149
The Negro Speaks of Rivers 149
Poem 150
Suicide's Note 151
Mother to Son 151
A House in Taos 152

GWENDOLYN B. BENNETT
Quatrains 155
Secret 155
Advice 156
To a Dark Girl 157
Your Songs 157
Fantasy 158
Lines Written at the Grave of Alexander Dumas 159
Hatred 160
Sonnet—1 160
Sonnet—2 161

ARNA BONTEMPS
The Return 163
A Black Man Talks of Reaping 165

To a Young Girl Leaving the Hill Country 165
Nocturne at Bethesda 166
Length of Moon 168
Lancelot 169
Gethsemane 169
A Tree Design 170
Blight 170
The Day-breakers 171
Close Your Eyes! 171
God Give to Men 172
Homing 172
Golgotha Is a Mountain 173

ALBERT RICE
The Black Madonna 177

COUNTEE CULLEN
Lines to Our Elders 179
I Have a Rendezvous with Life 180
Protest 181
Yet Do I Marvel 182
To Lovers of Earth: Fair Warning 182
From the Dark Tower 183
To John Keats, Poet, at Springtime 184
Four Epitaphs 186
Incident 187

DONALD JEFFREY HAYES
Inscription 188
Auf Wiedersehen 189
Night 189
Confession 190
Nocturne 190
After All 191

JONATHAN HENDERSON BROOKS
The Resurrection 193
The Last Quarter Moon of the Dying Year 195
Paean 195

GLADYS MAY CASELY HAYFORD
Nativity 197

CONTENTS

Rainy Season Love Song 198
The Serving Girl 200
Baby Cobina 200

LUCY ARIEL WILLIAMS
Northboun' 201

GEORGE LEONARD ALLEN
To Melody 204
Portrait 204

RICHARD BRUCE
Shadow 206
Cavalier 207

WARING CUNEY
The Death Bed 208
A Triviality 209
I Think I See Him There 210
Dust 210
No Images 212
The Radical 212
True Love 213

EDWARD S. SILVERA
South Street 214
Jungle Taste 214

HELENE JOHNSON
What Do I Care for Morning 216
Sonnet to a Negro in Harlem 217
Summer Matures 217
Poem 218
Fulfillment 219
The Road 221
Bottled 221
Magalu 223

WESLEY CURTWRIGHT
The Close of Day 225

LULA LOWE WEEDEN
Me Alone 227
Have You Seen It 228

Robin Red Breast 228
The Stream 228
The Little Dandelion 229
Dance 229
INDEX 230

PAUL LAURENCE DUNBAR

PAUL LAURENCE DUNBAR. Born, Dayton, Ohio, June 27, 1872. Educated in public schools, and graduated from Dayton High School, where he achieved some distinction. Editor of school paper, and noted as a versifier, from his grammar-school days. Printed his first book, *Oak and Ivy*, in 1893.

Two friends of his early manhood helped most to shape his career, and to encourage him in his days of struggle— Dr. H. A. Tobey, the celebrated alienist of Toledo, Ohio, and Frederick Douglass. The former helped him to bring his second book, *Majors and Minors*, before the public; the latter, with whom he was associated in the Negro Building at the World's Fair in Chicago in 1893, was the hero of the poet's dreams, the one to whom he dedicated two of his most serious poems.

Although Dunbar is remembered largely for his dialect verse, it was never his intention to concentrate on dialect. His poems in pure English constitute the greater bulk of his verse, and that to which he was most passionately devoted. The tragedy of his life was that the world "turned to praise the jingle in a broken tongue." His friendship for Booker Washington and a visit to Tuskegee inspired him to write the Tuskegee School Song, which is sung to the tune of "Fair Harvard."

The famous criticism of *Majors and Minors* by William Dean Howells in *Harper's Weekly*, June 27, 1897 established Dunbar's prestige as an important figure in American literature. From that time his success was assured.

He was married to Alice Ruth Moore of New Orleans, a teacher in Brooklyn, N. Y., in March, 1898.

1

He was as indefatigable a writer of prose as of poetry; short stories, novels, criticism, essays and some short plays poured from his pen.   His published works, exclusive of the two volumes of verse mentioned above, are: *Lyrics of Lowly Life, Lyrics of the Hearthside, Lyrics of Sunshine and Shadow;* several smaller volumes, illustrated editions of poems in the preceding volumes; short stories, *Folks from Dixie, The Strength of Gideon;* novels, *The Un-called, The Fanatics, The Love of Landry, The Sport of the Gods.*

He died in Dayton, Ohio, February 9, 1906.

Alice Dunbar Nelson.

ERE SLEEP COMES DOWN TO SOOTHE THE WEARY EYES[1]

ERE sleep comes down to soothe the weary eyes,
Which all the day with ceaseless care have sought
The magic gold which from the seeker flies;
Ere dreams put on the gown and cap of thought,
And make the waking world a world of lies,—
Of lies most palpable, uncouth, forlorn,
That say life's full of aches and tears and sighs,—
Oh, how with more than dreams the soul is torn,
Ere sleep comes down to soothe the weary eyes.

Ere sleep comes down to soothe the weary eyes,
How all the griefs and heartaches we have known
Come up like pois'nous vapors that arise
From some base witch's caldron, when the crone,

[1] Copyright 1896 by Dodd, Mead & Company, Inc.

To work some potent spell, her magic plies.
The past which held its share of bitter pain,
Whose ghost we prayed that Time might exorcise,
Comes up, is lived and suffered o'er again,
Ere sleep comes down to soothe the weary eyes.

Ere sleep comes down to soothe the weary eyes,
What phantoms fill the dimly lighted room;
What ghostly shades in awe-creating guise
Are bodied forth within the teeming gloom.
What echoes faint of sad and soul-sick cries,
And pangs of vague inexplicable pain
That pay the spirit's ceaseless enterprise,
Come thronging through the chambers of the brain,
Ere sleep comes down to soothe the weary eyes.

Ere sleep comes down to soothe the weary eyes,
Where ranges forth the spirit far and free?
Through what strange realms and unfamiliar skies
Tends her far course to lands of mystery?
To lands unspeakable—beyond surmise,
Where shapes unknowable to being spring,
Till, faint of wing, the Fancy fails and dies
Much wearied with the spirit's journeying,
Ere sleep comes down to soothe the weary eyes.

Ere sleep comes down to soothe the weary eyes,
How questioneth the soul that other soul,—
The inner sense which neither cheats nor lies,
But self exposes unto self, a scroll

Full writ with all life's acts unwise or wise,
In characters indelible and known;
So, trembling with the shock of sad surprise,
The soul doth view its awful self alone,
Ere sleep comes down to soothe the weary eyes.

When sleep comes down to seal the weary eyes,
The last dear sleep whose soft embrace is balm,
And whom sad sorrow teaches us to prize
For kissing all our passions into calm,
Ah, then, no more we heed the sad world's cries,
Or seek to probe th' eternal mystery,
Or fret our souls at long-withheld replies,
At glooms through which our visions cannot see,
When sleep comes down to seal the weary eyes.

DEATH SONG[1]

Lay me down beneaf de willers in de grass,
Whah de branch'll go a-singin' as it pass.
An' w'en I's a-layin' low,
I kin hyeah it as it go
Singin', "Sleep, my honey, tek yo' res' at las'."

Lay me nigh to whah hit meks a little pool,
An' de watah stan's so quiet lak an' cool,
Whah de little birds in spring,
Ust to come an' drink an' sing,
An' de chillen waded on dey way to school.

Let me settle w'en my shouldahs draps dey load
Nigh enough to hyeah de noises in de road;
   Fu' I t'ink de las' long res'
   Gwine to soothe my sperrit bes'
If I's layin' 'mong de t'ings I's allus knowed.

LIFE[1]

A CRUST of bread and a corner to sleep in,
A minute to smile and an hour to weep in,
A pint of joy to a peck of trouble,
And never a laugh but the moans come double:
      And that is life!

A crust and a corner that love makes precious,
With the smile to warm and the tears to refresh us:
And joy seems sweeter when cares come after,
And a moan is the finest of foils for laughter:
      And that is life!

AFTER THE QUARREL[2]

So WE, who've supped the self-same cup,
To-night must lay our friendship by;
Your wrath has burned your judgment up,
Hot breath has blown the ashes high.

You say that you are wronged—ah, well,
I count that friendship poor, at best
A bauble, a mere bagatelle,
That cannot stand so slight a test.

I fain would still have been your friend,
And talked and laughed and loved with you;
But since it must, why, let it end;
The false but dies, 'tis not the true.
So we are favored, you and I,
Who only want the living truth.
It was not good to nurse the lie;
'Tis well it died in harmless youth.

I go from you to-night to sleep.
Why, what's the odds? why should I grieve?
I have no fund of tears to weep
For happenings that undeceive.
The days shall come, the days shall go
Just as they came and went before.
The sun shall shine, the streams shall flow
Though you and I are friends no more.

And in the volume of my years,
Where all my thoughts and acts shall be,
The page whereon your name appears
Shall be forever sealed to me.
Not that I hate you over-much,
'Tis less of hate than love defied;

Howe'er, our hands no more shall touch,
We'll go our ways, the world is wide.

SHIPS THAT PASS IN THE NIGHT[1]

Out in the sky the great dark clouds are massing;
I look far out into the pregnant night,
Where I can hear a solemn booming gun
And catch the gleaming of a random light,
That tells me that the ship I seek is passing, passing.

My tearful eyes my soul's deep hurt are glassing;
For I would hail and check that ship of ships.
I stretch my hands imploring, cry aloud,
My voice falls dead a foot from mine own lips,
And but its ghost doth reach that vessel,
                    passing, passing.

O Earth, O Sky, O Ocean, both surpassing,
O heart of mine, O soul that dreads the dark!
Is there no hope for me? Is there no way
That I may sight and check that speeding bark
Which out of sight and sound is passing,
                    passing?

[1] Copyright 1896 by Dodd, Mead & Company, Inc.

WE WEAR THE MASK[1]

WE WEAR the mask that grins and lies,
It hides our cheeks and shades our eyes,—
This debt we pay to human guile;
With torn and bleeding hearts we smile,
And mouth with myriad subtleties.

Why should the world be over-wise,
In counting all our tears and sighs?
Nay, let them only see us, while
        We wear the mask.

We smile, but, O great Christ, our cries
To thee from tortured souls arise.
We sing, but oh the clay is vile
Beneath our feet, and long the mile;
But let the world dream otherwise,
        We wear the mask!

SYMPATHY[2]

I KNOW what the caged bird feels, alas!
When the sun is bright on the upland slopes;
When the wind stirs soft through the springing grass
And the river flows like a stream of glass;
When the first bird sings and the first bud opes,

And the faint perfume from its chalice steals—
I know what the caged bird feels!

I know why the caged bird beats his wing
Till its blood is red on the cruel bars;
For he must fly back to his perch and cling
When he fain would be on the bough a-swing;
And a pain still throbs in the old, old scars
And they pulse again with a keener sting—

I know why he beats his wing!
I know why the caged bird sings, ah me,
When his wing is bruised and his bosom sore,—
When he beats his bars and he would be free;
It is not a carol of joy or glee,
But a prayer that he sends from his heart's deep core,
But a plea, that upward to Heaven he flings—
I know why the caged bird sings!

THE DEBT [1]

THIS is the debt I pay
Just for one riotous day,
Years of regret and grief,
Sorrow without relief.

Pay it I will to the end—
Until the grave, my friend,

[1] Copyright 1896 by Dodd, Mead & Company, Inc.

Gives me a true release—
Gives me the clasp of peace.

Slight was the thing I bought,
Small was the debt I thought,
Poor was the loan at best—
God! but the interest!

JOSEPH S. COTTER, SR.

"I was born in Nelson County, Ky., February 2nd, 1861, on a farm owned by my great grandfather, Daniel Stapp, a tanner. In 1829 he bought himself and a part of his master's farm. Later he bought his daughter, Lucinda, my mother's mother.

Martha, my mother, was born on a nearby farm owned by her English-Indian father, Fleming Vaughan. Prior to my birth she lived in Bardstown and was a servant at "My Old Kentucky Home." She took me to Bardstown soon after my birth and brought me to Louisville in my fourth week, and here I have lived ever since.

I attended a private school and could read before my fourth year. Conditions were such that my attendance at school was very irregular. I quit school in my eighth year, having completed the third grade, and did not return until my twenty-second year.

During this time I picked up rags in the streets and worked in tobacco factories and brick-yards. My nineteenth year found me a distiller in one of the largest distilleries in Kentucky. A turn of fortune made me a teamster. I hauled cotton and tobacco and made up my mind to enter the prize ring. Another turn of fortune put me into a Louisville public night school. Here I began in the third grade where I left off in my eighth year.

At the end of two school sessions of five months each I was promoted to the high school. I keep this diploma under lock and key, for it is the only one I have ever received.

The man who turned my attention from prize-fighting to night school and then to school teaching, and who discovered my knack for writing verses, was Dr. W. T. Peyton of Louisville. He was my greatest benefactor.

My talent of whatever kind comes from Martha, my mother. She was poet, story-teller, dramatist and musician. My published works are: *A Rhyming, Links of Friendship, Caleb, the Degenerate*, a poetic drama, *A White Song And A Black One* and *Negro Tales*. My unpublished works are: *Life's Dawn And Dusk*, poems, *Caesar Driftwood and Other One Act Plays* and *My Mother And Her Family*.

THE TRAGEDY OF PETE

THERE was a man
  Whose name was Pete,
And he was a buck
  From his head to his feet.

He loved a dollar,
  But hated a dime;
And so was poor
  Nine-tenths of the time.

The Judge said "Pete,
  What of your wife?"

And Pete replied
  "She lost her life."

"Pete," said the Judge,
  "Was it lost in a row?
Tell me quick,
  And tell me how."

Pete straightened up
  With a hic and a sigh,
Then looked the Judge
  Full in the eye.

"O, Judge, my wife
  Would never go
To a Sunday dance
  Or a movie show.

"But I went, Judge,
  Both day and night,
And came home broke
  And also tight.

"The moon was up,
  My purse was down,
And I was the bully
  Of the bootleg town.

"I was crooning a lilt
  To corn and rye

For the loop in my legs
  And the fight in my eye.

"I met my wife;
  She was wearing a frown,
And catechising
  Her Sunday gown.

'O Pete, O Pete'
  She cried aloud,
'The Devil is falling
  Right out of a cloud.'

"I looked straight up
  And fell flat down
And a Ford machine
  Pinned my head to the ground.

"The Ford moved on,
  And my wife was in it;
And I was sober,
  That very minute.

"For my head was bleeding,
  My heart was a-flutter;
And the moonshine within me
  Was tipping the gutter.

"The Ford, it faster
  And faster sped

Till it dipped and swerved
And my wife was dead.

"Two bruised men lay
In a hospital ward—
One seeking vengeance,
The other the Lord.

"He said to me:
'Your wife was drunk,
You are crazy,
And my Ford is junk.'

"I raised my knife
And drove it in
At the top of his head
And the point of his chin.

"O Judge, O Judge,
If the State has a chair,
Please bind me in it
And roast me there."

There was a man
Whose name was Pete,
And he welcomed death
From his head to his feet.

THE WAY-SIDE WELL

A FANCY halts my feet at the way-side well.

It is not to drink, for they say the water is brackish.

It is not to tryst, for a heart at the mile's end beckons me on.

It is not to rest, for what feet could be weary when a heart at the mile's end keeps time with their tread?

It is not to muse, for the heart at the mile's end is food for my being.

I will question the well for my secret by dropping a pebble into it.

Ah, it is dry.

Strike lightning to the road, my feet, for hearts are like wells. You may not know they are dry 'til you question their depths.

Fancies clog the way to Heaven, and saints miss their crown.

JAMES WELDON JOHNSON

JAMES WELDON JOHNSON was born in Jacksonville, Fla. He graduated from Atlanta University with the degree of A. B., and he received the degree of A. M. from the same University in 1904. He spent three years in graduate work at Columbia University in the City of New York. The honorary degree of Litt.D. was conferred upon him by Talladega College, Talladega, Ala., in 1917, and by Howard University in 1923.

For several years Mr. Johnson was principal of the

colored high school at Jacksonville. He was admitted to
the Florida bar in 1897, and practiced law in Jacksonville,
until 1901, when he moved to New York to collaborate
with his brother, J. Rosamond Johnson, in writing for the
light opera stage.

In 1906, he was appointed United States Consul at
Puerto Cabello, Venezuela, being transferred as Consul to
Corinto, Nicaragua, in 1909. While in Corinto, he looked
after the interests of his country during the stormy days
of revolution which resulted in the downfall of Zelaya, and
through the abortive revolution against Diaz.

His knowledge of Spanish has been put to use in the
translation of a number of Spanish plays. He was the
translator for the English libretto of *Goyescas,* the Span-
ish grand opera produced by the Metropolitan Opera Com-
pany in 1915.

Mr. Johnson was for ten years the Contributing Editor
of the New York *Age.* He added to his distinction as a
newspaper writer by winning in an editorial contest one
of three prizes offered by the Philadelphia *Public Ledger*
in 1916. His poems have appeared in the *Century,* the
Independent, the *Crisis* and other publications.

In the spring of 1920, Mr. Johnson was sent by the
National Association for the Advancement of Colored
People to the black republic of Haiti, where he made an
investigation of U. S. misrule. The charges which Mr.
Johnson published in *The Nation,* of New York, upon his
return were taken up by Senator Harding, and as a con-
sequence a Naval Board of Inquiry was sent to Haiti and
a Congressional Investigation promised. The articles pub-
lished in *The Nation* have since been republished in a
pamphlet entitled, "Self-Determining Haiti."

Mr. Johnson is Secretary of the National Association
for the Advancement of Colored People, a member of the
Board of Directors of the American Fund for Public

Service (The Garland Fund), and a trustee of Atlanta
University.

Mr. Johnson's works include:
The Autobiography of an Ex-Colored Man
Fifty Years and Other Poems
English Libretto of "Goyescas"
The Book of American Negro Poetry
The Book of American Negro Spirituals
Second Book of Negro Spirituals
God's Trombones (Seven Negro Sermons in Verse)

FROM THE GERMAN OF UHLAND

THREE students once tarried over the Rhine,
And into Frau Wirthin's turned to dine.

"Say, hostess, have you good beer and wine?
And where is that pretty daughter of thine?"

"My beer and wine is fresh and clear.
My daughter lies on her funeral bier."

They softly tipped into the room;
She lay there in the silent gloom.

The first the white cloth gently raised,
And tearfully upon her gazed.

"If thou wert alive, O, lovely maid,
My heart at thy feet would to-day be laid!"

The second covered her face again,
And turned away with grief and pain.

"Ah, thou upon thy snow-white bier!
And I have loved thee so many a year."

The third drew back again the veil,
And kissed the lips so cold and pale.

"I've loved thee always, I love thee to-day,
And will love thee, yes, forever and aye!"

THE GLORY OF THE DAY WAS IN HER FACE

THE glory of the day was in her face,
The beauty of the night was in her eyes.
And over all her loveliness, the grace
Of Morning blushing in the early skies.

And in her voice, the calling of the dove;
Like music of a sweet, melodious part.
And in her smile, the breaking light of love;
And all the gentle virtues in her heart.

And now the glorious day, the beauteous night,
The birds that signal to their mates at dawn,
To my dull ears, to my tear-blinded sight
Are one with all the dead, since she is gone.

THE CREATION

(A Negro Sermon)

AND God stepped out on space,
And he looked around and said,
"I'm lonely—
I'll make me a world."

And far as the eye of God could see
Darkness covered everything,
Blacker than a hundred midnights
Down in a cypress swamp.

Then God smiled,
And the light broke,
And the darkness rolled up on one side,
And the light stood shining on the other,
And God said, *"That's good!"*

Then God reached out and took the light in His hands,
And God rolled the light around in His hands
Until He made the sun;
And He set that sun a-blazing in the heavens.
And the light that was left from making the sun
God gathered it up in a shining ball
And flung it against the darkness,
Spangling the night with the moon and stars.
Then down between

The darkness and the light
He hurled the world;
And God said, *"That's good!"*

Then God himself stepped down—
And the sun was on His right hand,
And the moon was on His left;
The stars were clustered about His head,
And the earth was under His feet.
And God walked, and where He trod
His footsteps hollowed the valleys out
And bulged the mountains up.

Then He stopped and looked and saw
That the earth was hot and barren.
So God stepped over to the edge of the world
And He spat out the seven seas;
He batted His eyes, and the lightnings flashed;
He clapped His hands, and the thunders rolled;
And the waters above the earth came down,
The cooling waters came down.

Then the green grass sprouted,
And the little red flowers blossomed,
The pine tree pointed his finger to the sky,
And the oak spread out his arms,
The lakes cuddled down in the hollows of the ground,
And the rivers ran down to the sea;
And God smiled again,

And the rainbow appeared,
And curled itself around His shoulder.

Then God raised His arm and He waved His hand
Over the sea and over the land,
And He said, "*Bring forth!   Bring forth!*"
And quicker than God could drop His hand,
Fishes and fowls
And beasts and birds
Swam the rivers and the seas,
Roamed the forests and the woods,
And split the air with their wings.
And God said, "*That's good!*"

Then God walked around,
And God looked around
On all that He had made.
He looked at His sun,
And He looked at His moon,
And He looked at His little stars;
He looked on His world
With all its living things,
And God said, "*I'm lonely still.*"

Then God sat down
On the side of a hill where He could think;
By a deep, wide river He sat down;
With His head in His hands,
God thought and thought,
Till He thought, "*I'll make me a man!*"

Up from the bed of the river
God scooped the clay;
And by the bank of the river
He kneeled Him down;
And there the great God Almighty
Who lit the sun and fixed it in the sky,
Who flung the stars to the most far corner of the night,
Who rounded the earth in the middle of His hand;
This Great God,
Like a mammy bending over her baby,
Kneeled down in the dust
Toiling over a lump of clay
Till He shaped it in His own image;

Then into it He blew the breath of life,
And man became a living soul.
Amen.   Amen.

THE WHITE WITCH

O BROTHERS mine, take care!   Take care!
The great white witch rides out to-night.
Trust not your prowess nor your strength,
Your only safety lies in flight;
For in her glance is a snare,
And in her smile there is a blight.

The great white witch you have not seen?
Then, younger brothers mine, forsooth,

Like nursery children you have looked
For ancient hag and snaggle-tooth;
But no, not so; the witch appears
In all the glowing charms of youth.

Her lips are like carnations, red,
Her face like new-born lilies, fair,
Her eyes like ocean waters, blue,
She moves with subtle grace and air,
And all about her head there floats
The golden glory of her hair.

But though she always thus appears
In form of youth and mood of mirth,
Unnumbered centuries are hers,
The infant planets saw her birth;
The child of throbbing Life is she,
Twin sister to the greedy earth.

And back behind those smiling lips,
And down within those laughing eyes,
And underneath the soft caress
Of hand and voice and purring sighs,
The shadow of the panther lurks,
The spirit of the vampire lies.

For I have seen the great white witch,
And she has led me to her lair,
And I have kissed her red, red lips
And cruel face so white and fair;

Around me she has twined her arms,
And bound me with her yellow hair.

I felt those red lips burn and sear
My body like a living coal;
Obeyed the power of those eyes
As the needle trembles to the pole;
And did not care although I felt
The strength go ebbing from my soul.

Oh! she has seen your strong young limbs,
And heard your laughter loud and gay,
And in your voices she has caught
The echo of a far-off day,
When man was closer to the earth;
And she has marked you for her prey.

She feels the old Antaean strength
In you, the great dynamic beat
Of primal passions, and she sees
In you the last besieged retreat
Of love relentless, lusty, fierce,
Love pain-ecstatic, cruel-sweet.

O, brothers mine, take care! Take care!
The great white witch rides out to-night.
O, younger brothers mine, beware;
Look not upon her beauty bright;
For in her glance there is a snare,
And in her smile there is a blight.

MY CITY

WHEN I come down to sleep death's endless night,
The threshold of the unknown dark to cross,
What to me then will be the keenest loss,
When this bright world blurs on my fading sight?
Will it be that no more I shall see the trees
Or smell the flowers or hear the singing birds
Or watch the flashing streams or patient herds?
No, I am sure it will be none of these.

But, ah! Manhattan's sights and sounds, her smells,
Her crowds, her throbbing force, the thrill that comes
From being of her a part, her subtile spells,
Her shining towers, her avenues, her slums—
O God! the stark, unutterable pity,
To be dead, and never again behold my city!

WILLIAM EDWARD BURGHARDT DU BOIS

I WAS born in Massachusetts and educated in her schools,
at Fisk University, at Harvard and Berlin. My first pub-
lished writings were news notes in *The New York Age*.
Then I had an article in *The Atlantic Monthly* and in 1896
my doctor's thesis on the slave trade was published as my
first book. *The Souls of Black Folk* appeared in 1903
and one or two other books thereafter. I taught at Wil-
berforce, Pennsylvania and Atlanta and became editor of
The Crisis in 1910.

A LITANY OF ATLANTA[1]

Done at Atlanta, in the Day of Death, 1906.

O SILENT God, Thou whose voice afar in mist and mystery hath left our ears an-hungered in these fearful days—
Hear us, good Lord!

Listen to us, Thy children: our faces dark with doubt are made a mockery in Thy sanctuary. With uplifted hands we front Thy heaven, O God crying:
We beseech Thee to hear us, good Lord!

We are not better than our fellows, Lord, we are but weak and human men. When our devils do deviltry, curse Thou the doer and the deed: curse them as we curse them, do to them all and more than ever they have done to innocence and weakness, to womanhood and home.
Have mercy upon us, miserable sinners!

And yet whose is the deeper guilt? Who made these devils? Who nursed them in crime and fed them on injustice? Who ravished and debauched their mothers and their grandmothers? Who bought and sold their crime, and waxed fat and rich on public iniquity?
Thou knowest, good God!

[1] From "Dark Water" by W. E. B. Du Bois, Copyright 1920 by Harcourt, Brace & Company, Inc.

Is this Thy Justice, O Father, that guile be easier than innocence, and the innocent crucified for the guilt of the untouched guilty?

Justice, O Judge of men!

Wherefore do we pray? Is not the God of the fathers dead? Have not seers seen in Heaven's halls Thine hearsed and lifeless form stark amidst the black and rolling smoke of sin, where all along bow bitter forms of endless dead?

Awake, Thou that sleepest!

Thou art not dead, but flown afar, up hills of endless light, thru blazing corridors of suns, where worlds do swing of good and gentle men, of women strong and free —far from the cozenage, black hypocrisy and chaste prostitution of this shameful speck of dust!

Turn again, O Lord, leave us not to perish in our sin!

From lust of body and lust of blood
Great God, deliver us!

From lust of power and lust of gold,
Great God, deliver us!

From the leagued lying of despot and of brute,
Great God, deliver us!

A city lay in travail, God our Lord, and from her loins sprang twin Murder and Black Hate. Red was the midnight; clang, crack and cry of death and fury filled the air and trembled underneath the stars when church spires pointed silently to Thee. And all this was to sate the greed of greedy men who hide behind the veil of vengeance!

Bend us Thine ear, O Lord!

In the pale, still morning we looked upon the deed. We stopped our ears and held our leaping hands, but they—did they not wag their heads and leer and cry with bloody jaws: *Cease from Crime!* The word was mockery, for thus they train a hundred crimes while we do cure one.

Turn again our captivity, O Lord!

Behold this maimed and broken thing; dear God, it was an humble black man who toiled and sweat to save a bit from the pittance paid him. They told him: *Work and Rise.* He worked. Did this man sin? Nay, but some one told how some one said another did—one whom he had never seen nor known. Yet for that man's crime this man lieth maimed and murdered, his wife naked to shame, his children, to poverty and evil.

Hear us, O Heavenly Father!

Doth not this justice of hell stink in Thy nostrils, O God? How long shall the mounting flood of innocent blood roar in Thine ears and pound in our hearts for vengeance? Pile the pale frenzy of blood-crazed brutes

who do such deeds high on Thine altar, Jehovah Jireh, and burn it in hell forever and forever!
Forgive us, good Lord; we know not what we say!

Bewildered we are, and passion-tost, mad with the madness of a mobbed and mocked and murdered people; straining at the armposts of Thy Throne, we raise our shackled hands and charge Thee, God, by the bones of our stolen fathers, by the tears of our dead mothers, by the very blood of Thy crucified Christ: *What meaneth this?* Tell us the Plan; give us the Sign!
Keep not Thou silence, O God!

Sit no longer blind, Lord God, deaf to our prayer and dumb to our dumb suffering. Surely, Thou too art not white, O Lord, a pale, bloodless, heartless thing?
Ah! Christ of all the Pities!

Forgive the thought! Forgive these wild, blasphemous words. Thou art still the God of our black fathers, and in Thy soul's soul sit some soft darkenings of the evening, some shadowings of the velvet night.

But whisper—speak—call, great God, for Thy silence is white terror to our hearts! The way, O God, show us the way and point us the path.

Whither? North is greed and South is blood; within, the coward, and without the liar. Whither? To death?
Amen! Welcome dark sleep!

Whither? To life? But not this life, dear God, not this. Let the cup pass from us, tempt us not beyond our strength, for there is that clamoring and clawing within, to whose voice we would not listen, yet shudder lest we must, and it is red, Ah! God! It is a red and awful shape.

Selah!

In yonder East trembles a star.
Vengeance is mine; I will repay, saith the Lord!

Thy will, O Lord, be done!
Kyrie Eleison!

Lord, we have done these pleading, wavering words.
We beseech Thee to hear us, good Lord!

We bow our heads and hearken soft to the sobbing of women and little children.
We beseech Thee to hear us, good Lord!

Our voices sink in silence and in night.
Hear us, good Lord!

In night, O God of a godless land!
Amen!

In silence, O Silent God.
Selah!

WILLIAM STANLEY BRAITHWAITE

WILLIAM STANLEY BRAITHWAITE was born in Boston Dec. 6, 1878. He inherited the incentives and ideals of the intellect from an ancestry of British gentlemen. He has written verse and prose and was for many years leading reviewer of books in the *Boston Transcript*. He has published twenty volumes, and his yearly anthology of verse establishes for each year the best poetry printed in the magazines.

SCINTILLA

I KISSED a kiss in youth
    Upon a dead man's brow;
And that was long ago,—
    And I'm a grown man now.

It's lain there in the dust,
    Thirty years and more;—
My lips that set a light
    At a dead man's door.

RYE BREAD

FATHER JOHN's bread was made of rye,
Felicite's bread was white;
Father John loved the sun noon-high,
Felicite, the moon at night.

Father John drank wine with his bread;
Felicite drank sweet milk;
Father John loved flowers, pungent and red;
Felicite, lilies soft as silk.

Father John's soul was made of bronze,
That God's salt was corroding;
Felicite's soul was a wind that runs
With a blue flame of foreboding.

Between these two was the shadow of a dome
That cut their lives in twain;
But Dionysus led them home
In a chariot of pain.

OCTOBER XXIX, 1795

(Keats' Birthday)

TIME sitting on the throne of Memory
Bade all her subject Days the past had known
Arise and say what thing gave them renown
Unforgetable, 'Rising from the sea,
I gave the Genoese his dreams to be;'
'I saw the Corsican's Guards swept down;'
'Colonies I made free from a tyrant's crown;'—
So each Day told its immortality.

And with these blazing triumphs spoke one voice

Whose wistful speech no vaunting did employ:
'I know not if 'twere by Fate's chance or choice
I hold the lowly birth of an English boy;
I only know he made man's heart rejoice
Because he played with Beauty for a toy!'

DEL CASCAR

Del Cascar, Del Cascar
Stood upon a flaming star,
Stood and let his feet hang down
Till in China the toes turned brown.

And he reached his fingers over
The rim of the sea, like sails from Dover,
And caught a Mandarin at prayer,
And tickled his nose in Orion's hair.

The sun went down through crimson bars,
And left his blind face battered with stars—
But the brown toes in China kept
Hot the tears Del Cascar wept.

JAMES EDWARD McCALL

James Edward McCall was born September 2, 1880 at
Montgomery, Ala., and received his early education in the
public schools of that city. Graduating from the Alabama
State Normal in 1900 he entered Howard University as

a medical student the same year, but some months later was forced to abandon his medical career, following an attack of typhoid fever leading to total blindness. Undaunted by this misfortune, he at once set out to develop his literary talent. During this period he read and studied much through the eyes of others, also writing many poems, a number of which were published in Southern dailies, the *New York World* and other periodicals. *The Montgomery* (Alabama) *Advertiser* styled him "The Blind Tom of Literature." One of his poems, *"Meditation,"* has been compared to Bryant's "Thanatopsis."

Despite his handicap, McCall determined to acquire a college education. Accompanied by his sister, he entered Albion College (Michigan) in 1905, where he was graduated two years later, being the only sightless student in the college. Returning to his natal city, he took up journalistic work, for some years being employed as a special writer for one of the local white dailies, also contributing to other periodicals, and ultimately publishing at Montgomery a successful race weekly—*The Emancipator.*

This blind writer is ably assisted in his journalistic work by his wife, to whom he was married in 1914. He and his family moved to Detroit in 1920. He is city editor and editorial writer for the *Detroit Independent,* his editorials in this publication having been widely read and re-published throughout the country during the past two years.

THE NEW NEGRO

HE SCANS the world with calm and fearless eyes,
  Conscious within of powers long since forgot;
At every step, new man-made barriers rise

To bar his progress—but he heeds them not.
He stands erect, though tempests round him crash,
  Though thunder bursts and billows surge and roll;
He laughs and forges on, while lightnings flash
  Along the rocky pathway to his goal.
Impassive as a Sphinx, he stares ahead—
  Foresees new empires rise and old ones fall;
While caste-mad nations lust for blood to shed,
  He sees God's finger writing on the wall.
With soul awakened, wise and strong he stands,
Holding his destiny within his hands.

ANGELINA WELD GRIMKÉ

ANGELINA WELD GRIMKÉ was born in Boston, Mass., February 27, 1880. She was a student at Carleton Academy, Northfield, Minn., Cushing Academy, Ashburnham, Mass., and Girls' Latin School, Boston. In 1902 she was graduated from the Boston Normal School of Gymnastics. In 1902 she began her career as a teacher in the Armstrong Manual Training School in Washington, D. C.; since 1916 she has taught in the Dunbar High School in the same city. She is the author of a three act play *Rachel* published in 1920, short stories, and numerous poems.

HUSHED BY THE HANDS OF SLEEP

(To Dr. George F. Grant)

I

Hushed by the hands of Sleep,
  By the beautiful hands of Sleep.
Very gentle and quiet he lies,
With a little smile of sweet surprise,
Just softly hushed at lips and eyes,
  Hushed by the hands of Sleep,
    By the beautiful hands of Sleep.

II

Hushed by the hands of Sleep,
  By the beautiful hands of Sleep.
Death leaned down as his eyes grew dim,
And his face, I know, was not strange, not grim,
But oh! it was beautiful to him,
  Hushed by the hands of Sleep,
    By the beautiful hands of Sleep.

GREENNESS

Tell me is there anything lovelier,
  Anything more quieting

Than the green of little blades of grass
And the green of little leaves?

Is not each leaf a cool green hand,
Is not each blade of grass a mothering green finger,
Hushing the heart that beats and beats and beats?

THE EYES OF MY REGRET

ALWAYS at dusk, the same tearless experience,
The same dragging of feet up the same well-worn path
To the same well-worn rock;
The same crimson or gold dropping away of the sun,
The same tints—rose, saffron, violet, lavender, grey,
Meeting, mingling, mixing mistily;
Before me the same blue black cedar rising jaggedly to
        a point;
Over it, the same slow unlidding of twin stars,
Two eyes unfathomable, soul-searing,
Watching, watching—watching me;
The same two eyes that draw me forth, against my will
        dusk after dusk;
The same two eyes that keep me sitting late into the
        night, chin on knees,
Keep me there lonely, rigid, tearless, numbly miserable,
        —The eyes of my Regret.

GRASS FINGERS

Touch me, touch me,
Little cool grass fingers,
Elusive, delicate grass fingers.
With your shy brushings,
Touch my face—
My naked arms—
My thighs—
My feet.
Is there nothing that is kind?
You need not fear me.
Soon I shall be too far beneath you,
For you to reach me, even,
With your tiny, timorous toes.

SURRENDER

We ask for peace.   We, at the bound
O life, are weary of the round
In search of Truth.   We know the quest
Is not for us, the vision blest
Is meant for other eyes.   Uncrowned,
We go, with heads bowed to the ground,
And old hands, gnarled and hard and browned.
Let us forget the past unrest,—
       We ask for peace.

Our strainéd ears are deaf,—no sound
May reach them more; no sight may wound
Our worn-out eyes. We gave our best,
And, while we totter down the West,
Unto that last, that open mound,—
            We ask for peace.

THE WAYS O' MEN

'Tis queer, it is, the ways o' men,
Their comin's and their goin's;
For there's the grey road,
    The straight road
With the grey dust liftin'
    With ev'ry step
And the little roads off-flingin'.

Maybe it's a bit of a sly field
That crooks a finger to them
And sends them to the turnin';
Or the round firm bosom
    Of a little hill
Acallin' to them, them with their heads
        That heavy;
Or maybe it's the black look
    Given out of the tail of the eye;
Or a white word, wingin';
Maybe it's only the back of a little tot's neck
  In the sunlight;

Or the red lips of a woman
   Parting slow. . . .
Sure there's no tellin'.

One I saw goin' towards a white star
   At the edge of a daffydill sky,
   Its lights kissin' straight into his eyes.
Maybe it's a gold piece
To be taken from another
   In the dark;
Or the neat place between the ribs
Waitin' for the knife
That one comes after carryin' for it.
'Tis few, it is, that goes with the grey road
   The straight road
   All the way,
With the grey dust liftin' at ev'ry step.

'Tis queer, it is, the ways o' men,
With a level look at you, or a crooked
   As they be passin'.
                    Pouf!
Sure, 'tis so fast they're goin',
Does it matter about the turnin's?

TENEBRIS

THERE is a tree, by day,
That, at night,

Has a shadow,
A hand huge and black,
With fingers long and black.
   All through the dark,
Against the white man's house,
   In the little wind,
The black hand plucks and plucks
   At the bricks.
The bricks are the color of blood and very small.
   Is it a black hand,
   Or is it a shadow?

WHEN THE GREEN LIES OVER
THE EARTH

WHEN the green lies over the earth, my dear,
A mantle of witching grace,
When the smile and the tear of the young child year
Dimple across its face,
And then flee, when the wind all day is sweet
With the breath of growing things,
When the wooing bird lights on restless feet
And chirrups and trills and sings
          To his lady-love
          In the green above,
Then oh! my dear, when the youth's in the year,

Yours is the face that I long to have near,
        Yours is the face, my dear.

But the green is hiding your curls, my dear,
Your curls so shining and sweet;
And the gold-hearted daisies this many a year
Have bloomed and bloomed at your feet,
And the little birds just above your head
With their voices hushed, my dear,
For you have sung and have prayed and have pled
        This many, many a year.

        And the blossoms fall,
        On the garden wall,
And drift like snow on the green below.
        But the sharp thorn grows
        On the budding rose,
And my heart no more leaps at the sunset glow.
For oh! my dear, when the youth's in the year,
Yours is the face that I long to have near,
Yours is the face, my dear.

A MONA LISA

1.

I SHOULD like to creep
Through the long brown grasses
    That are your lashes;

I should like to poise
        On the very brink
Of the leaf-brown pools
        That are your shadowed eyes;
I should like to cleave
        Without sound,
Their glimmering waters,
        Their unrippled waters,
I should like to sink down
        And down
            And down . . . .
                And deeply drown.

2.

Would I be more than a bubble breaking?
        Or an ever-widening circle
        Ceasing at the marge?
Would my white bones
        Be the only white bones
Wavering back and forth, back and forth
        In their depths?

PARADOX

WHEN face to face we stand
        And eye to eye,
How far apart we are——

As far, they say, as God can ever be
From what, they say, is Hell.

. . . . .

But, when we stand
Fronting the other,
Mile after mile slipping in between,
O, close we are,
As close as is the shadow to the body,
As breath, to life, ...
As kisses are to love.

. . . . .

YOUR HANDS

I love your hands:
They are big hands, firm hands, gentle hands;
Hair grows on the back near the wrist . . . .
I have seen the nails broken and stained
From hard work.
And yet, when you touch me,
I grow small . . . . and quiet . . . . . .
. . . . And happy . . . .
If I might only grow small enough
To curl up into the hollow of your palm,
Your left palm,
Curl up, lie close and cling,

So that I might know myself always there,
. . . . Even if you forgot.

I WEEP

— I weep —
Not as the young do noisily,
Not as the aged rustily,
But quietly.
Drop by drop the great tears
Splash upon my hands,
And save you saw them shine,
You would not know
I wept.

FOR THE CANDLE LIGHT

THE sky was blue, so blue that day
And each daisy white, so white,
O, I knew that no more could rains fall grey
And night again be night.

. . . . .

I *knew*, I *knew*. Well, if night is night,
And the grey skies greyly cry,
I have in a book for the candle light,
A daisy dead and dry.

DUSK

Twin stars through my purpling pane,
    The shriveling husk
Of a yellowing moon on the wane—
    And the dusk.

THE PUPPET PLAYER

Sometimes it seems as though some puppet player
    A clenched claw cupping a craggy chin,
Sits just beyond the border of our seeing,
    Twitching the strings with slow sardonic grin.

A WINTER TWILIGHT

A silence slipping around like death,
Yet chased by a whisper, a sigh, a breath;
One group of trees, lean, naked and cold,
Inking their crests 'gainst a sky green-gold;
One path that knows where the corn flowers were;
Lonely, apart, unyielding, one fir;
And over it softly leaning down,
One star that I loved ere the fields went brown.

ANNE SPENCER

From Lynchburg, Va., where she lives, Anne Spencer
writes, "Mother Nature, February, forty-five years ago
forced me on the stage that I, in turn, might assume the
rôle of lonely child, happy wife, perplexed mother—and,
so far, a twice resentful grandmother. I have no academic
honors, nor lodge regalia. I am a Christian by intention,
a Methodist by inheritance, and a Baptist by marriage. I
write about some of the things I love. But have no civil-
ized articulation for the things I hate. I proudly love
being a Negro woman—its so involved and interesting.
We are the PROBLEM—the great national game of
TABOO."

NEIGHBORS

Ah, you are cruel;
You ask too much;
Offered a hand, a finger-tip,
You must have a soul to clutch.

I HAVE A FRIEND

I have a friend
And my heart from hence
Is closed to friendship,
Nor the gods' knees hold but one;
He watches with me thru the long night,
And when I call he comes,
Or when he calls I am there;

He does not ask me how beloved
Are my husband and children,
Nor ever do I require
Details of life and love
In the grave—his home,—
We are such friends.

SUBSTITUTION

Is LIFE itself but many ways of thought,
Does *thinking* furl the poets' pleiades,
Is in His slightest convolution wrought
These mantled worlds and their men-freighted seas?
He thinks—and being comes to ardent things:
The splendor of the day-spent sun, love's birth,—
Or dreams a little, while creation swings
The circle of His mind and Time's full girth . . .
As here within this noisy peopled room
My thought leans forward . . . quick! you're lifted
    clear
Of brick and frame to moonlit garden bloom,—
Absurdly easy, now, our walking, dear,
Talking, my leaning close to touch your face . . .
His All-Mind bids us keep this sacred place!

QUESTING

LET me learn now where Beauty is;
My day is spent too far toward night

To wander aimlessly and miss her place;
To grope, eyes shut, and fingers touching space.

Her maidens I have known, seen durance beside,
Handmaidens to the Queen, whose duty bids
Them lie and lure afield their Vestal's acolyte,
Lest a human shake the throne, lest a god should know
    his might:
Nereid, daughter of the Trident, steering in her shell,
Paused in voyage, smile beguiling, tempted and I fell;
Spiteful dryads, sport forsaking, tossing birchen
    wreathes,
Left the Druidic priests they teased so
In the oaken trees, crying, "Ho a mortal! here a be-
    liever!"
Bound me, she who held the sceptre, stricken by her,
    ah, deceiver . . .
But let me learn now where Beauty is;
I was born to know her mysteries,
And needing wisdom I must go in vain:
Being sworn bring to some hither land,
Leaf from her brow, light from her torchéd hand.

LIFE-LONG, POOR BROWNING . . .

LIFE-LONG, poor Browning never knew Virginia,
Or he'd not grieved in Florence for April sallies
Back to English gardens after Euclid's linear:
Clipt yews, Pomander Walks, and pleachéd alleys;

Primroses, prim indeed, in quite ordered hedges,
Waterways, soberly, sedately enchanneled,
No thin riotous blade even among the sedges,
All the wild country-side tamely impaneled . . .

Dead, now, dear Browning, lives on in heaven,—
(Heaven's Virginia when the year's at its Spring)
He's haunting the byways of wine-aired leaven
And throating the notes of the wildings on wing;

Here canopied reaches of dogwood and hazel,
Beech tree and redbud fine-laced in vines,
Fleet clapping rills by lush fern and basil,
Drain blue hills to lowlands scented with pines . . .

Think you he meets in this tender green sweetness
Shade that was Elizabeth . . . immortal completeness!

DUNBAR

Ah, how poets sing and die!
Make one song and Heaven takes it;
Have one heart and Beauty breaks it;
Chatterton, Shelley, Keats and I—
Ah, how poets sing and die!

INNOCENCE

SHE tripped and fell against a star,
A lady we all have known;
Just what the villagers lusted for
To claim her one of their own;
Fallen but once the lower felt she,
So turned her face and died,—
With never a hounding fool to see
'Twas a star-lance in her side!

CREED

IF MY garden oak spares one bare ledge
For a boughed mistletoe to grow and wedge;
And all the wild birds this year should know
I cherish their freedom to come and go;
If a battered worthless dog, masterless, alone,
Slinks to my heels, sure of bed and bone;
And the boy just moved in, deigns a glance-assay,
Turns his pockets inside out, calls, "Come and play!"
If I should surprise in the eyes of my friend
That the deed was *my* favor he'd let me lend;
Or hear it repeated from a foe I despise,
That I whom he hated was chary of lies;
If a pilgrim stranger, fainting and poor,
Followed an urge and rapped at my door,
And my husband loves me till death puts apart,
Less as flesh unto flesh, more as heart unto heart:

I may challenge God when we meet That Day,
And He dare not be silent or send me away.

LINES TO A NASTURTIUM
(A lover muses)

FLAME-FLOWER, Day-torch, Mauna Loa,
I saw a daring bee, today, pause, and soar,
    Into your flaming heart;
Then did I hear crisp, crinkled laughter
As the furies after tore him apart?
    A bird, next, small and humming,
Looked into your startled depths and fled. . . . .
Surely, some dread sight, and dafter
    Than human eyes as mine can see,
Set the stricken air waves drumming
    In his flight.

Day-torch, Flame-flower, cool-hot Beauty,
I cannot see, I cannot hear your flutey
Voice lure your loving swain,
But I know one other to whom you are in beauty
Born in vain:
Hair like the setting sun,
Her eyes a rising star,
Motions gracious as reeds by Babylon, bar
All your competing;
Hands like, how like, brown lilies sweet,
Cloth of gold were fair enough to touch her feet . . .

Ah, how the sense floods at my repeating,
As once in her fire-lit heart I felt the furies
Beating, beating.

AT THE CARNIVAL

GAY little Girl-of-the-Diving-Tank,
I desire a name for you,
Nice, as a right glove fits;
For you—who amid the malodorous
Mechanics of this unlovely thing,
Are darling of spirit and form.
I know you—a glance, and what you are
Sits-by-the-fire in my heart.
My Limousine-Lady knows you, or
Why does the slant-envy of her eye mark
Your straight air and radiant inclusive smile?
Guilt pins a fig-leaf; Innocence is its own adorning.
The bull-necked man knows you—this first time
His itching flesh sees form divine and vibrant health,
And thinks not of his avocation.
I came incuriously—
Set on no diversion save that my mind
Might safely nurse its brood of misdeeds
In the presence of a blind crowd.
The color of life was gray.
Everywhere the setting seemed right
For my mood!
Here the sausage and garlic booth

Sent unholy incense skyward;
There a quivering female-thing
Gestured assignations, and lied
To call it dancing;
There, too, were games of chance
With chances for none;
But oh! the Girl-of-the-Tank, at last!
Gleaming Girl, how intimately pure and free
The gaze you send the crowd,
As though you know the dearth of beauty
In its sordid life.
We need you—my Limousine-Lady,
The bull-necked man, and I.
Seeing you here brave and water-clean,
Leaven for the heavy ones of earth,
I am swift to feel that what makes
The plodder glad is good; and
Whatever is good is God.
The wonder is that you are here;
I have seen the queer in queer places,
But never before a heaven-fed
Naiad of the Carnival-Tank!
Little Diver, Destiny for you,
Like as for me, is shod in silence;
Years may seep into your soul
The bacilli of the usual and the expedient;
I implore Neptune to claim his child to-day!

MARY EFFIE LEE NEWSOME

BORN in Philadelphia January 19, 1885. Daughter of
Bishop B. F. and Mrs. Mary Elizabeth Lee. Reared in
Ohio, at Wilberforce. Married 1920, Rev. Henry Nesby
Newsome. Is a lover of the out-of-doors, and of the
beautiful.

MORNING LIGHT[1]

(The Dew-Drier)

BROTHER to the firefly—
For as the firefly lights the night,
So lights he the morning—
Bathed in the dank dews as he goes forth
Through heavy menace and mystery
Of half-waking tropic dawn,
Behold a little boy,
A naked black boy,
Sweeping aside with his slight frame
Night's pregnant tears,
And making a morning path to the light
For the tropic traveler!

2

Bathed in the blood of battle,
Treading toward a new morning,

---

[1] (This poem, published in the CRISIS during the World War, was written after reading
an account of the little African babies who are sent before the explorer into jungle grasses
that tower many feet. The little boys, Dan Crawford says in his THINKING BLACK,
who go out to tread down a path and by chance meet the lurking leopard or hyena are
"Human Brooms," and are called DEW-DRIERS.)

May not his race—
Its body long bared to the world's disdain,
Its face schooled to smile for a light to come—
May not his race, even as the Dew Boy leads,
Bear onward the world to a time
When tolerance, forbearance,
Such as reigned in the heart of ONE
Whose heart was gold
Shall shape the world for that fresh dawning
After the dews of blood?

PANSY

OH, THE blue blue bloom
On the velvet cheek
Of the little pansy's face
That hides away so still and cool
In some soft garden place!
The tiger lily's orange fires,
The red lights from the rose
Aren't like the gloom on that blue cheek
Of the softest flower that grows!

SASSAFRAS TEA

THE sass'fras tea is red and clear
In my white china cup,

So pretty I keep peeping in
Before I drink it up.

I stir it with a silver spoon,
And sometimes I just hold
A little tea inside the spoon,
Like it was lined with gold.

It makes me hungry just to smell
The nice hot sass'fras tea,
And that's one thing I really like
That they say's good for me.

SKY PICTURES

SOMETIMES a right white mountain
Or great soft polar bear,
Or lazy little flocks of sheep
Move on in the blue air.
The mountains tear themselves like floss,
The bears all melt away.
The little sheep will drift apart
In such a sudden way.
And then new sheep and mountains come.
New polar bears appear
And roll and tumble on again
Up in the skies so clear.
The polar bears would like to get
Where polar bears belong.

The mountains try so hard to stand
In one place firm and strong.
The little sheep all want to stop
And pasture in the sky,
But never can these things be done,
Although they try and try!

THE QUILT

I HAVE the greatest fun at night,
When casement windows are all bright.
I make believe each one's a square
Of some great quilt up in the air.

The blocks of gold have black between,
Wherever only night is seen.
It surely makes a mammoth quilt—
With bits of dark and checks of gilt—
To cover up the tired day
In such a cozy sort of way.

THE BAKER'S BOY

THE baker's boy delivers loaves
All up and down our street.
His car is white, his clothes are white,
White to his very feet.
I wonder if he stays that way.

I don't see how he does all day.
I'd like to watch him going home
When all the loaves are out.
His clothes must look quite different then,
At least I have no doubt.

WILD ROSES

WHAT! Roses growing in a meadow
Where all the cattle browse?
I'd think they'd fear the very shadow
Of daddy's big rough cows.

QUOITS

IN wintertime I have such fun
When I play quoits with father.
I beat him almost every game.
He never seems to bother.

He looks at mother and just smiles.
All this seems strange to me,
For when he plays with grown-up folks,
He beats them easily.

JOHN   FREDERICK   MATHEUS

"I was born September 10, 1887, in Keyser, West Virginia.   My early education was received in Steubenville, Ohio, my mother's home.   I was graduated from High School in 1905.   For one year thereafter I was bookkeeper and helper in a plumbing shop.

Proceeding to Cleveland, Ohio, I entered Adelbert College of Western Reserve University.   In 1910 I won the A.B. degree *cum laude* and a wife.

I lived for a time in Philadelphia then began service in the Florida Agricultural and Mechanical College at Tallahassee, as teacher, first of Mathematics, then of Latin and English.   Later I became Professor of Romance Languages.   During the war and after, I served as the college auditor and secretary.

In 1921 I received the M.A. Degree from Columbia University and the Teachers College Diploma as teacher of French.   In 1922 I became professor of Romance Languages in the West Virginia Collegiate Institute, Institute, West Virginia.

In 1924 I traveled in Cuba; in 1925 I studied at the University of Paris during the summer and toured Switzerland, Italy and southern France.

My interest in letters began early in grammar school days.   The daily papers of my home town used to print my puerile efforts when copy ran low.

Recently I have been the recipient of prizes and mention in the three annual *Opportunity* Literary Contests and in the 1926 *Crisis* contest, for short stories, personal sketches, a play and poems.   The 1925 *Opportunity* prize story 'Fog' is published in the *New Negro,* edited by Alain Locke."

REQUIEM

SHE wears, my beloved, a rose upon her head.
Walk softly angels, lest your gentle tread
Awake her to the turmoil and the strife,
The dissonance and hates called life.

She sleeps, my beloved, a rose upon her head.
Who says she will not hear, that she is dead?
The rose will fade and lose its lovely hue,
But not, my beloved, will fading wither you.

FENTON JOHNSON

"I CAME into the world May 7, 1888. No notice was taken of the event save in immediate circles. I presume the world was too busy or preoccupied to note it. It happened in Chicago. I went to school and also college. My scholastic record never attained me any notoriety.

Taught school one year and repented. Having scribbled since the age of nine, had some plays produced on the stage of the old Pekin Theatre, Chicago, at the time I was nineteen. When I was twenty-four my first volume *A Little Dreaming* was published. Since then *Visions of the Dusk* (1915) and *Songs of the Soil* (1916) represent my own collections of my work. Also published a volume of short stories *Tales of Darkest America* and a group of essays on American politics *For the Highest Good.* Work in poetry appears in the following anthologies: *The New Poetry* (Monroe and Henderson), *Victory* (Braithwaite), *Others* (Kreymborg), *The Chicago Anthology* (Blanden), *Anthology of Magazine Verse* (Braithwaite),

Poetry by American Negroes (White and Jackson), *Negro Poets and their Poetry* (Kerlin), *Poets of America* (Wood), *Book of American Negro Poetry* (J. W. Johnson), *Today's Poetry* (Crawford and O'Neil) and others.

Edited two or three magazines and published one or two of them myself.

My complete autobiography I promise to the world when I am able to realize that I have done something."

WHEN I DIE

WHEN I die my song shall be
Crooning of the summer breeze;
When I die my shroud shall be
Leaves plucked from the maple trees;
On a couch as green as moss
And a bed as soft as down,
I shall sleep and dream my dream
Of a poet's laurel crown.

When I die my star shall drop
Singing like a nightingale;
When I die my soul shall rise
Where the lyre-strings never fail;
In the rose my blood shall lie,
In the violet the smile,
And the moonbeams thousand strong
Past my grave each night shall file.

PUCK GOES TO COURT

I WENT to court last night,
Before me firefly light;
And there was Lady Mab,
On cheek a cunning dab
Of rouge the sun sent down,
King Oberon with crown
Of gold eyed daisy buds
Among potato spuds
Was dancing roundelay
With Lady Chloe and May.

I hid among the flowers
And spent the wee young hours
In mixing up the punch;
For I was on a hunch
That sober men are dull
And fairy dust will lull
To rest the plodding mind
Worn down by life's thick grind.

The nobles drank the brew
And called it sweetest dew;
But when I left they lay
Stunned by the light of day
And Oberon had writ
Decree that I must flit
A hundred leagues from court.
(Alas! Where is there sport?)

THE MARATHON RUNNER

If I have run my course and seek the pearls
My Psyche fain would drink at Mermelon
And rest content in wine and nectar cup
Who knows but that the gods have found me whole
And in their stewardship of man would bless
The sweating lover fickle man once knew?

I know that I might pull the tendon bands
That hold my soul together—ay, might bend
Each nerve and muscle spirit fain would keep—
That I might hear the maddening cheers of men
Who when the morrow dawns forget the games
And cast instead the dice in market place.

But I have found sweeter peace than fame;
And in the evening dwell on heights divine,
Betwixt my lips a rose from Cupid's hands,
Upon my brow the laurel Belvidere
Entwines from tree beside the throne of Zeus
And flowing from my speech Athene's words
Dipped long in wisdom's fount to heal the soul.

JESSIE FAUSET

"Philadelphia where I was born and educated was once
the dear delight of my heart. But everything in my life
has contrived to pull me away from it. First I travelled

to Cornell University and came back with a Phi Beta Kappa key and a degree of Bachelor of Arts. That launched me. Since then I've seen England, Scotland, France, Belgium, Switzerland, Italy, Austria and Algeria. The College de France and the Alliance Francaise have given me some points on the difference between the French of Stratford-atte-Bowe and that of Paris. And there was a pleasant year too at the University of Pennsylvania when I renewed my acquaintance with Philadelphia and earned a Master's Degree. So much for education. As to occupations I've taught Latin and French in the Dunbar High School in Washington, D. C. And served as Literary Editor on the *Crisis* in New York.

Wonderful days those! Now I'm teaching French again in the City of New York which at present claims my love and allegiance. Like the French I am fond of dancing, and adore cards and the theatre probably because I am a minister's daughter. All my life I have wanted to write novels and have had one published. But usually, in spite of myself, I have scribbled poetry. . . . I should like to see the West Indies, South America and Tunis and live a long time on the French Riviera. Aside from this I have few desires. And I find life perpetually enchanting."

WORDS! WORDS!

How did it happen that we quarreled?
We two who loved each other so!
Only the moment before we were one,
Using the language that lovers know.
And then of a sudden, a word, a phrase
That struck at the heart like a poignard's blow.
And you went berserk, and I saw red,

And love lay between us, bleeding and dead!
Dead! When we'd loved each other so!

How *could* it happen that we quarreled!
Think of the things we used to say!
"What does it matter, dear, what you do?
Love such as ours has to last for aye!"
—"Try me! I long to endure your test!"
—"Love, we shall always love, come what may!"
What are the words the apostle saith?
"In the power of the tongue are Life and Death!"
Think of the things we used to say!

TOUCHE

DEAR, when we sit in that high, placid room,
"Loving" and "doving" as all lovers do,
Laughing and leaning so close in the gloom,—

What is the change that creeps sharp over you?
Just as you raise your fine hand to my hair,
Bringing that glance of mixed wonder and rue?

"Black hair," you murmur, "so lustrous and rare,
Beautiful too, like a raven's smooth wing;
Surely no gold locks were ever more fair."

Why do you say every night that same thing?
Turning your mind to some old constant theme,
Half meditating and half murmuring?

Tell me, that girl of your young manhood's dream,
Her you loved first in that dim long ago—
Had *she* blue eyes? Did *her* hair goldly gleam?

Does *she* come back to you softly and slow,
Stepping wraith-wise from the depths of the past?
Quickened and fired by the warmth of our glow?

There I've divined it! My wit holds you fast.
Nay, no excuses; 'tis little I care.
I knew a lad in my own girlhood's past,—
Blue eyes he had and such waving gold hair!

NOBLESSE OBLIGE

LOLOTTE, who attires my hair,
Lost her lover. Lolotte weeps;
Trails her hand before her eyes;
Hangs her head and mopes and sighs,
Mutters of the pangs of hell.
Fills the circumambient air
With her plaints and her despair.
Looks at me:
"May you never know, Mam'selle,
Love's harsh cruelty."

Love's dart lurks in my heart too,—
None may know the smart
Throbbing underneath my smile.

Burning, pricking all the while
That I dance and sing and spar,
Juggling words and making quips
To hide the trembling of my lips.
I must laugh
What time I moan to moon and star
To help me stand the gaff.

What a silly thing is pride!
Lolotte bares her heart.
Heedless that each runner reads
All her thoughts and all her needs.
What I hide with my soul's life
Lolotte tells with tear and cry.
Blurs her pain with sob and sigh.
Happy Lolotte, she!
I must jest while sorrow's knife
Stabs in ecstasy.

"If I live, I shall outlive."
Meanwhile I am barred
From expression of my pain.
Let my heart be torn in twain,
Only I may know the truth.
Happy Lolotte, blessed she
Who may tell her agony!
On me a seal is set.
Love is lost, and—bitter ruth—
Pride is with me yet!

LA VIE C'EST LA VIE

On summer afternoons I sit
Quiescent by you in the park,
And idly watch the sunbeams gild
And tint the ash-trees' bark.

Or else I watch the squirrels frisk
And chaffer in the grassy lane;
And all the while I mark your voice
Breaking with love and pain.

I know a woman who would give
Her chance of heaven to take my place;
To see the love-light in your eyes,
The love-glow on your face!

And there's a man whose lightest word
Can set my chilly blood afire;
Fulfilment of his least behest
Defines my life's desire.

But he will none of me. Nor I
Of you. Nor you of her. 'Tis said
The world is full of jests like these.—
I wish that I were dead.

THE RETURN

I THAT had found the way so smooth
With gilly-flowers that beck and nod,
Now find that same road wild and steep
With need for compass and for rod.
And yet with feet that bleed, I pant
On blindly,—stumbling back to God!

RENCONTRE

MY HEART that was so passionless
Leapt high last night when I saw you!
Within me surged the grief of years
And whelmed me with its endless rue.
My heart that slept so still, so spent,
Awoke last night,—to break anew!

FRAGMENT

THE breath of life imbued those few dim days!
Yet all we had was this,—
A flashing smile, a touch of hands, and once
A fleeting kiss.

Blank futile death inheres these years between!
Still naught have you and I

But frozen tears, and stifled words, and once
A sharp caught cry.

ALICE DUNBAR NELSON

BORN Alice Ruth Moore, in New Orleans, Louisiana.
Educated in public schools and Straight College in New
Orleans.   Afterwards studied at University of Pennsyl-
vania, Cornell University and School of Industrial Art.
Married to Paul Laurence Dunbar in 1898.   Taught
school prior to marriage in New Orleans, and Brooklyn.
One of the founders of the White Rose Industrial Home
in New York, and the Industrial School for Colored Girls
in Delaware.   At present teaching in Delaware.

Published *Violets and Other Tales, The Goodness of
St. Rocque, Masterpieces of Negro Eloquence, The Dun-
bar Speaker,* and *The Negro in Louisiana.*   Contributor
to magazines and newspapers, as short story writer and
columnist.

Married to Robert John Nelson, 1916.

SNOW IN OCTOBER

TODAY I saw a thing of arresting poignant beauty:
A strong young tree, brave in its Autumn finery
Of scarlet and burnt umber and flame yellow,
Bending beneath a weight of early snow,
Which sheathed the north side of its slender trunk,
And spread a heavy white chilly afghan
Over its crested leaves.

Yet they thrust through, defiant, glowing,
Claiming the right to live another fortnight,
Clamoring that Indian Summer had not come,
Crying "Cheat! Cheat!" because Winter had stretched
Long chill fingers into the brown, streaming hair
Of fleeing October.

The film of snow shrouded the proud redness of the tree,
As premature grief grays the strong head
Of a virile, red-haired man.

SONNET

I HAD no thought of violets of late,
The wild, shy kind that spring beneath your feet
In wistful April days, when lovers mate
And wander through the fields in raptures sweet.
The thought of violets meant florists' shops,
And bows and pins, and perfumed papers fine;
And garish lights, and mincing little fops
And cabarets and songs, and deadening wine.
So far from sweet real things my thoughts had strayed,
I had forgot wide fields, and clear brown streams;
The perfect loveliness that God has made,—
Wild violets shy and Heaven-mounting dreams.
And now—unwittingly, you've made me dream
Of violets, and my soul's forgotten gleam.

I SIT AND SEW

I SIT and sew—a useless task it seems,
My hands grown tired, my head weighed down with
    dreams—
The panoply of war, the martial tread of men,
Grim-faced, stern-eyed, gazing beyond the ken
Of lesser souls, whose eyes have not seen Death
Nor learned to hold their lives but as a breath—
But—I must sit and sew.

I sit and sew—my heart aches with desire—
That pageant terrible, that fiercely pouring fire
On wasted fields, and writhing grotesque things
Once men. My soul in pity flings
Appealing cries, yearning only to go
There in that holocaust of hell, those fields of woe—
But—I must sit and sew.—

The little useless seam, the idle patch;
Why dream I here beneath my homely thatch,
When there they lie in sodden mud and rain,
Pitifully calling me, the quick ones and the slain?
You need me, Christ! It is no roseate dream
That beckons me—this pretty futile seam,
It stifles me—God, must I sit and sew?

GEORGIA DOUGLAS JOHNSON

MANY years ago a little yellow girl in Atlanta, Georgia, came across a poem in a current paper that told of a rose struggling to bloom in a window in New York City. A child tended this flower and her whole life was wrapt up in its fate. This poem was written by William Stanley Braithwaite, years before the world knew how marvellous was his mind. Some one told the reader of these lines that the writer was colored and straightway she began to walk upward toward him.

This little girl grew up, went to Atlanta University, Oberlin Conservatory, taught school, then married Henry Lincoln Johnson, always looking forward toward the light of the poet Braithwaite.

Then her husband was appointed Recorder of Deeds under Taft and she was moved by circumstances to the capital—Washington.

Dean Kelly Miller at Howard University saw some of her poetic efforts and was pleased. Stanley Braithwaite was his friend and he directed her to send something to him at Boston. She did so, and then began a quickening and a realization that she could do!

Following this happy event, Dr. W. E. B. Du Bois of the *Crisis* brought out two poems from her pen that awakened the interest of readers.

At this time Jessie Fauset, the novelist, was teaching French in Washington and very generously helped her to gather together material for her first book *The Heart of A Woman* with an introduction by William Stanley Braithwaite. This was followed by *Bronze,* a book of color with an introduction by W. E. B. Du Bois. Her third attempt in poetry was *An Autumn Love Cycle* with an introduction by Alain Locke, the editor of *The New Negro.*

At present she is connected with the Department of

Labor at Washington, as Commissioner of Conciliation.
At her home there you may find the young writers gathered
together almost any Saturday night exchanging ideas, re-
citing new poems or discussing plans for new creations.

SERVICE

WHEN we count out our gold at the end of the day,
And have filtered the dross that has cumbered the way,
Oh, what were the hold of our treasury then
Save the love we have shown to the children of men?

HOPE

FRAIL children of sorrow, dethroned by a hue,
The shadows are flecked by the rose sifting through,
The world has its motion, all things pass away,
No night is omnipotent, there must be day.

The oak tarries long in the depth of the seed,
But swift is the season of nettle and weed,
Abide yet awhile in the mellowing shade,
And rise with the hour for which you were made.

The cycle of seasons, the tidals of man
Revolve in the orb of an infinite plan,
We move to the rhythm of ages long done,
And each has his hour—to dwell in the sun!

THE SUPPLIANT

Long have I beat with timid hands upon life's leaden
    door,
Praying the patient, futile prayer my fathers prayed
    before,
Yet I remain without the close, unheeded and unheard,
And never to my listening ear is borne the waited word.

Soft o'er the threshold of the years there comes this
    counsel cool:
The strong demand, contend, prevail; the beggar is a
    fool!

LITTLE SON

The very acme of my woe,
    The pivot of my pride,
My consolation, and my hope
    Deferred, but not denied.
The substance of my every dream,
    The riddle of my plight,
The very world epitomized
    In turmoil and delight.

OLD BLACK MEN

THEY have dreamed as young men dream
　　Of glory, love and power;
They have hoped as youth will hope
　　Of life's sun-minted hour.

They have seen as others saw
　　Their bubbles burst in air,
And they have learned to live it down
　　As though they did not care.

LETHE

I DO not ask for love, ah! no,
　　Nor friendship's happiness,
These were relinquished long ago;
　　I search for something less.

I seek a little tranquil bark
　　In which to drift at ease
Awhile, and then quite silently
　　To sink in quiet seas.

PROVING

WERE you a leper bathed in wounds
　　And by the world denied;

I'd share your fatal exile
As a privilege and pride.
You are to me the sun, the moon,
The starlight of my soul,
The sounding motif of my heart,
The impetus and goal!

I WANT TO DIE WHILE YOU LOVE ME

I WANT to die while you love me,
While yet you hold me fair,
While laughter lies upon my lips
And lights are in my hair.

I want to die while you love me
And bear to that still bed
Your kisses turbulent, unspent
To warm me when I'm dead.

I want to die while you love me;
Oh, who would care to live
Till love has nothing more to ask
And nothing more to give?

I want to die while you love me,
And never, never see
The glory of this perfect day
Grow dim, or cease to be!

RECESSIONAL

CONSIDER me a memory, a dream that passed away;
Or yet a flower that has blown and shattered in a day;
For passion sleeps alas and keeps no vigil with the years
And wakens to no conjuring of orisons or tears.

Consider me a melody that served its simple turn,
Or but the residue of fire that settles in the urn,
For love defies pure reasoning and undeterred flows
Within, without, the vassal heart—its reasoning who
    knows?

MY LITTLE DREAMS

I'M folding up my little dreams
   Within my heart tonight,
And praying I may soon forget
   The torture of their sight.

For time's deft fingers scroll my brow
   With fell relentless art—
I'm folding up my little dreams
   Tonight, within my heart.

WHAT NEED HAVE I FOR MEMORY?

WHAT need have I for memory,
  When not a single flower
Has bloomed within life's desert
  For me, one little hour?

What need have I for memory
  Whose burning eyes have met
The corse of unborn happiness
  Winding the trail regret?

WHEN I AM DEAD

WHEN I am dead, withhold, I pray, your blooming
    legacy;
Beneath the willows did I bide, and they should cover
    me;
I longed for light and fragrance, and I sought them far
    and near,
O, it would grieve me utterly, to find them on my bier!

THE DREAMS OF THE DREAMER

THE dreams of the dreamer
  Are life-drops that pass

    The break in the heart
      To the soul's hour-glass.

    The songs of the singer
      Are tones that repeat
    The cry of the heart
      Till it ceases to beat.

THE HEART OF A WOMAN

THE heart of a woman goes forth with the dawn,
As a lone bird, soft winging, so restlessly on,
Afar o'er life's turrets and vales does it roam
In the wake of those echoes the heart calls home.

The heart of a woman falls back with the night,
And enters some alien cage in its plight,
And tries to forget it has dreamed of the stars
While it breaks, breaks, breaks on the sheltering bars.

CLAUDE McKAY

"I WAS born in a very little village high up in the
hills of the parish of Clarendon in the island of Jamaica.
The village was so small it hadn't a name like the larger

surrounding villages. But our place was called Sunny
Ville. I was the youngest of eleven.

My father was a peasant proprietor who owned his land
and cultivated large tracts of coffee, cocoa, bananas and
sugar-cane. When I was of school age I was sent to my
brother who was a schoolmaster in a small town in the
North-Western part of the island. He educated me. He
was a free-thinker and I became one, too, so soon as I
could think about life and religion. I was never a child
of any church. My brother had a nice library with books
of all sorts and I read such free-thought writers as
Haeckel, Huxley, Matthew Arnold, side by side with
Shakespeare and the great English novelists and poets
(excepting Browning) before I was fourteen. At that
time Shakespeare to me was only a wonderful story-teller.
When I was seventeen I won a Jamaica Government Trade
Scholarship and was apprenticed to a cabinet-maker and
wheelwright. I hated trade and quit. When I was nine-
teen I joined the Jamaica Constabulary and left it after
ten months. An English gentleman who was collecting
Jamaica folklore became interested in my dialect verses
and helped me to publish my first book: *Songs of Jamaica,*
in 1911. I was twenty years old then. The next year
I went to the United States. First to an educational insti-
tution for Negroes in the South. I did not like it, and
left there after three months for a college in a Western
state. There I stayed two years. Came to New York.
Abandoned all thought of returning to the West Indies.
Lost a few thousand dollars (a legacy) in high living and
bad business. Went to work at various jobs, porter,
houseman, longshoreman, bar-man, railroad club and hotel
waiter. Kept on writing. The *Seven Arts Magazine* took
two of my poems in 1917. In 1918 Frank Harris pub-
lished some poems in *Pearson's*. In 1919 *The Liberator*
published some things. The same year I went to Holland,
Belgium and England. Lived in London over a year.

Published *Spring in New Hampshire*. Returned to America in 1921. Got a job with Max Eastman on the *Liberator*. Kept it till Max Eastman left for Europe. Went to Russia in 1922. *Harlem Shadows* published 1922 by Harcourt, Brace & Co. Stayed six months in Moscow and Petrograd. Berlin in 1923. Paris at the end of 1923, where I was very ill for months. Been in France ever since trying to exist and write."

AMERICA[1]

ALTHOUGH she feeds me bread of bitterness,
And sinks into my throat her tiger's tooth,
Stealing my breath of life, I will confess
I love this cultured hell that tests my youth!
Her vigor flows like tides into my blood,
Giving me strength erect against her hate.
Her bigness sweeps my being like a flood.
Yet as a rebel fronts a king in state,
I stand within her walls with not a shred
Of terror, malice, not a word of jeer.
Darkly I gaze into the days ahead,
And see her might and granite wonders there,
Beneath the touch of Time's unerring hand,
Like priceless treasures sinking in the sand.

Claude McKay

[1] From "Harlem Shadows" by Claude McKay, Copyright 1922, by Harcourt, Brace & Company, Inc.

EXHORTATION: SUMMER, 1919[1]

THROUGH the pregnant universe rumbles life's terrific
　　thunder,
　And Earth's bowels quake with terror; strange and
　　terrible storms break,
Lightning-torches flame the heavens, kindling souls of
　　men, thereunder:
　Africa! long ages sleeping, O my motherland, awake!

In the East the clouds glow crimson with the new dawn
　　that is breaking,
　And its golden glory fills the western skies.
　O my brothers and my sisters, wake! arise!
For the new birth rends the old earth and the very dead
　　are waking,
　Ghosts are turned flesh, throwing off the grave's
　　disguise,
　And the foolish, even children, are made wise;
For the big earth groans in travail for the strong, new
　　world in making—
　O my brothers, dreaming for dim centuries,
　Wake from sleeping; to the East turn, turn your
　　eyes!

Oh the night is sweet for sleeping, but the shining day's
　　for working;

1 From "Harlem Shadows" by Claude McKay, Copyright 1922, by Harcourt, Brace &
Company, Inc.

Sons of the seductive night, for your children's children's sake,
From the deep primeval forests where the crouching leopard's lurking,
Lift your heavy-lidded eyes, Ethiopia! awake!

In the East the clouds glow crimson with the new dawn that is breaking,
And its golden glory fills the western skies.
O my brothers and my sisters, wake! arise!
For the new birth rends the old earth and the very dead are waking,
Ghosts are turned flesh, throwing off the grave's disguise,
And the foolish, even children, are made wise;
For the big earth groans in travail for the strong, new world in making—
O my brothers, dreaming for long centuries,
Wake from sleeping; to the East turn, turn your eyes!

FLAME-HEART[1]

So MUCH have I forgotten in ten years,
  So much in ten brief years! I have forgot
What time the purple apples come to juice,
  And what month brings the shy forget-me-not.

[1] From "Harlem Shadows" by Claude McKay, Copyright 1922, by Harcourt, Brace & Company, Inc.

I have forgot the special, startling season
   Of the pimento's flowering and fruiting;
What time of year the ground doves brown the fields
   And fill the noonday with their curious fluting.
I have forgotten much, but still remember
The poinsettia's red, blood-red in warm December.

I still recall the honey-fever grass,
   But cannot recollect the high days when
We rooted them out of the ping-wing path
   To stop the mad bees in the rabbit pen.
I often try to think in what sweet month
   The languid painted ladies used to dapple
The yellow by-road mazing from the main,
   Sweet with the golden threads of the rose-apple.
I have forgotten—strange—but quite remember
The poinsettia's red, blood-red in warm December.

What weeks, what months, what time of the mild year
   We cheated school to have our fling at tops?
What days our wine-thrilled bodies pulsed with joy
   Feasting upon blackberries in the copse?
Oh, some I know! I have embalmed the days,
   Even the sacred moments when we played,
All innocent of passion, uncorrupt,
   At noon and evening in the flame-heart's shade.
We were so happy, happy, I remember,
Beneath the poinsettia's red in warm December.

THE WILD GOAT[1]

O you would clothe me in silken frocks
   And house me from the cold,
And bind with bright bands my glossy locks,
   And buy me chains of gold.

And give me—meekly to do my will—
   The hapless sons of men:—
But the wild goat bounding on the barren hill
   Droops in the grassy pen.

RUSSIAN CATHEDRAL

Bow down my soul in worship very low
And in the holy silences be lost.
Bow down before the marble man of woe,
Bow down before the singing angel host.
What jewelled glory fills my spirit's eye!
What golden grandeur moves the depths of me!
The soaring arches lift me up on high
Taking my breath with their rare symmetry.

Bow down my soul and let the wondrous light
Of beauty bathe thee from her lofty throne,

[1] From "Harlem Shadows" by Claude McKay, Copyright 1922, by Harcourt, Brace & Company, Inc.

Bow down before the wonder of man's might.
Bow down in worship, humble and alone;
Bow lowly down before the sacred sight
Of man's divinity alive in stone.

DESOLATE

My SPIRIT is a pestilential city,
With misery triumphant everywhere,
Glutted with baffled hopes and lost to pity;
Strange agonies make quiet lodgment there.
Its bursting sewers ooze up from below,
And spread their loathsome substance through its lanes,
Flooding all areas with their evil flow,
And blocking all the motion of its veins.
Its life is sealed to love or hope or pity;
My spirit is a pestilential city.

Above its walls the air is heavy-wet,
Brooding in fever mood and hanging thick
Round empty tower and broken minaret,
Settling upon the tree-tops stricken sick
And withered in its dank contagious breath;
Their leaves are shrivelled silver, parched decay,
Like wilting creepers trailing underneath
The chalky yellow of a tropic way.
Round crumbling tower and leaning minaret,
The air hangs fever-filled and heavy-wet.

And all its many fountains no more spurt;
Within the dammed-up tubes they tide and foam
Around the drifting sludge and silted dirt,
And weep against the soft and liquid loam,
And so the city's ways are washed no more;
All is neglected and decayed within.
Clean waters beat against its high-walled shore
In furious force, but cannot enter in.
The suffocated fountains cannot spurt;
They foam and weep against the silted dirt.

Beneath the ebon gloom of mounting rocks
The little pools lie poisonously still.
And birds come to the edge in forlorn flocks,
And utter sudden plaintive notes and shrill,
Pecking at fatty grey-green substances;
But never do they dip their bills and drink.
They twitter sad, beneath the mournful trees,
And fretfully flit to and from the brink,
In little dull brown, green-and-purple flocks,
Beneath the jet-gloom of the mounting rocks.

And green-eyed moths of curious design,
With gold-black wings and brightly silver-dotted,
On nests of flowers among those rocks recline—
Bold, burning blossoms, strangely leopard-spotted,
But breathing deadly poison at the lips.
Oh, every lovely moth that wanders by,
And on the blossoms fatal nectar sips,
Is doomed in drooping stupor there to die—

All green-eyed moths of curious design
That on the fiercely-burning rocks recline.

Oh cold as death is all the loveliness
That breathes out of the strangeness of the scene,
And sickening like a skeleton's caress,
With clammy clinging fingers, long and lean.
Above it float a host of yellow flies,
Circling in changeless motion in their place,
Snow-thick and mucid in the drooping skies,
Swarming across the glassy floor of space.
Oh cold as death is all the loveliness
And sickening like a skeleton's caress.

There was a time when, happy with the birds,
The little children clapped their hands and laughed;
And midst the clouds the glad winds heard their words,
And blew down all the merry ways to waft
Their music to the scented fields of flowers.
Oh sweet were children's voices in those days,
Before the fall of pestilential showers,
That drove them forth from all the city's ways.
Now never, never more their silver words
Will mingle with the golden of the birds.

Gone, gone forever the familiar forms
To which my spirit once so dearly clung,
Blown worlds beyond by the destroying storms,

And lost away like lovely songs unsung.
Yet life still lingers, questioningly strange,
Timid and quivering, naked and alone,
Biding the cycle of disruptive change,
Though all the fond familiar forms are gone
Forever gone, the fond familiar forms,
Blown worlds beyond by the destroying storms.

ABSENCE[1]

YOUR words dropped into my heart like pebbles into a
    pool,
Rippling around my breast and leaving it melting cool.

Your kisses fell sharp on my flesh like dawn-dews from
    the limb
Of a fruit-filled lemon tree when the day is young and
    dim.

Like soft rain-christened sunshine, as fragile as rare
    gold lace,
Your breath, sweet-scented and warm, has kindled my
    tranquil face.

But a silence vasty-deep, oh deeper than all these ties
Now, through the menacing miles, brooding between
    us lies.

[1] From *Harlem Shadows* by Claude McKay, Copyright 1922, by Harcourt, Brace & Company, Inc.

And more than the songs I sing, I await your written
    word,
To stir my fluent blood as never your presence stirred.

MY HOUSE

For this peculiar tint that paints my house
Peculiar in an alien atmosphere
Where other houses wear a kindred hue,
I have a stirring always very rare
And romance-making in my ardent blood,
That channels through my body like a flood.

I know the dark delight of being strange,
The penalty of difference in the crowd,
The loneliness of wisdom among fools,
Yet never have I felt but very proud,
Though I have suffered agonies of hell,
Of living in my own peculiar cell.

There is an exaltation of man's life,
His hidden life, that he alone can feel.
The blended fires that heat his veins within,
Shaping his metals into finest steel,
Are elements from his own native earth,
That the wise gods bestowed on him at birth.

Oh each man's mind contains an unknown realm
Walled in from other men however near,

And unimagined in their highest flights
Of comprehension or of vision clear;
A realm where he withdraws to contemplate
Infinity and his own finite state.

Thence he may sometimes catch a god-like glimpse
Of mysteries that seem beyond life's bar;
Thence he may hurl his little shaft at heaven
And bring down accidentally a star,
And drink its foamy dust like sparkling wine
And echo accents of the laugh divine.

Then he may fall into a drunken sleep
And wake up in his same house painted blue
Or white or green or red or brown or black—
His house, his own, whatever be the hue.
But things for him will not be what they seem
To average men since he has dreamt his dream!

JEAN TOOMER

Jean Toomer was born in Washington, D. C., in 1894. He has since lived there and in New York, receiving his education mainly in these cities. Having traveled over a good part of America, experiencing varied aspects of its life and studying the elements of contemporary problems, in 1918 in the midst of a general interest in art, he gradually centered on that of literature. There followed a four year period devoted entirely to writing, the results of which were first given printed form by *The Double*

Dealer of New Orleans.   And soon thereafter, sketches, poems, short stories, and critical reviews began appearing in *Broom, The Crisis, The Dial, The Liberator, The Little Review, Opportunity,* etc.   These brought him in contact with a literary and artistic group in New York composed of such men as Waldo Frank, Alfred Steiglitz, Paul Rosenfeld, Gorham B. Munson, and others.   With these he has been associated in the effort to articulate the diverse significances of America.   In 1923 his first book, *Cane,* was published by Boni and Liveright, New York.

REAPERS

BLACK reapers with the sound of steel on stones
Are sharpening scythes.   I see them place the hones
In their hip-pockets as a thing that's done,
And start their silent swinging, one by one.
Black horses drive a mower through the weeds,
And there, a field rat, startled, squealing bleeds,
His belly close to ground.   I see the blade,
Blood-stained, continue cutting weeds and shade.

EVENING SONG

FULL moon rising on the waters of my heart,
Lakes and moon and fires,
Cloine tires,
Holding her lips apart.

Promises of slumber leaving shore to charm the moon,
Miracle made vesper-keeps,
Cloine sleeps,
And I'll be sleeping soon.

Cloine, curled like the sleepy waters where the moon-
    waves start,
Radiant, resplendently she gleams,
Cloine dreams,
Lips pressed against my heart.

GEORGIA DUSK

THE sky, lazily disdaining to pursue
    The setting sun, too indolent to hold
    A lengthened tournament for flashing gold,
Passively darkens for night's barbecue,

A feast of moon and men and barking hounds,
    An orgy for some genius of the South
    With blood-hot eyes and cane-lipped scented mouth,
Surprised in making folk-songs from soul sounds.

The sawmill blows its whistle, buzz-saws stop,
    And silence breaks the bud of knoll and hill,
    Soft settling pollen where plowed lands fulfill
Their early promise of bumper crop.

Smoke from the pyramidal sawdust pile
   Curls up, blue ghosts of trees, tarrying low
   Where only chips and stumps are left to show
The solid proof of former domicile.

Meanwhile, the men, with vestiges of pomp,
   Race memories of king and caravan,
   High-priests, an ostrich, and a juju-man,
Go singing through the footpaths of the swamp.

Their voices rise . . . the pine trees are guitars,
   Strumming, pine-needles fall like sheets of rain . . .
   Their voices rise . . . the chorus of the cane
Is caroling a vesper to the stars . . .

O singers, resinous and soft your songs
   Above the sacred whisper of the pines,
   Give virgin lips to cornfield concubines,
Bring dreams of Christ to dusky cane-lipped throngs.

SONG OF THE SON

   Pour O pour that parting soul in song,
   O pour it in the sawdust glow of night,
   Into the velvet pine-smoke air to-night,
   And let the valley carry it along.
   And let the valley carry it along.

O land and soil, red soil and sweet-gum tree,
So scant of grass, so profligate of pines,
Now just before an epoch's sun declines,
Thy son, in time, I have returned to thee,
Thy son, I have in time returned to thee.

In time, for though the sun is setting on
A song-lit race of slaves, it has not set;
Though late, O soil, it is not too late yet
To catch thy plaintive soul, leaving, soon gone,
Leaving, to catch thy plaintive soul soon gone.

O Negro slaves, dark purple ripened plums,
Squeezed, and bursting in the pine-wood air,
Passing, before they stripped the old tree bare
One plum was saved for me, one seed becomes

An everlasting song, a singing tree,
Caroling softly souls of slavery,
What they were, and what they are to me,
Caroling softly souls of slavery.

COTTON SONG

COME, brother, come. Let's lift it;
Come now, hewit! roll away!
Shackles fall upon the Judgment Day
But let's not wait for it.

God's body's got a soul,
Bodies like to roll the soul,
Can't blame God if we don't roll,
Come, brother, roll, roll!

Cotton bales are the fleecy way
Weary sinner's bare feet trod,
Softly, softly to the throne of God,
"We ain't agwine t' wait until th' Judgment Day!

Nassur; nassur,
Hump.
Eoho, eoho, roll away!
We ain't agwine t' wait until th' Judgment Day!"

God's body's got a soul,
Bodies like to roll the soul,
Can't blame God if we don't roll,
Come, brother, roll, roll!

FACE

HAIR—
silver-gray,
like streams of stars,
Brows—
recurved canoes
quivered by the ripples blown by pain,
Her eyes—

mist of tears
condensing on the flesh below
And her channeled muscles
are cluster grapes of sorrow
purple in the evening sun
nearly ripe for worms.

NOVEMBER COTTON FLOWER

BOLL-WEEVIL's coming, and the winter's cold,
Made cotton-stalks look rusty, seasons old,
And cotton, scarce as any southern snow,
Was vanishing; the branch, so pinched and slow,
Failed in its function as the autumn rake;
Drouth fighting soil had caused the soil to take
All water from the streams; dead birds were found
In wells a hundred feet below the ground—
Such was the season when the flower bloomed.
Old folks were startled, and it soon assumed
Significance. Superstition saw
Something it had never seen before:
Brown eyes that loved without a trace of fear,
Beauty so sudden for that time of year.

JOSEPH S. COTTER, JR.

"AT Thanksgiving time 1894 Paul Laurence Dunbar,
the Negro poet, was a guest in my house in Louisville, Ky.

Here for the first time in the South he read the Negro dialect poems that afterwards made him famous.

September 2nd, 1895, my son, the late Joseph S. Cotter, Jr., was born in the room in which these poems were read. He learned to read and write from his sister, Florence Olivia, who was two years older. Before he entered school at the age of six years he had read about thirty books— these included all the readers in the elementary schools— 1-2-3-4-5-6-7-8th grades and parts of the Bible.

Mrs. Maria F. Cotter, my wife, and I held both children back. We refused to allow them to be promoted in several instances. Both were graduated from the Louisville Central High School under 16; Florence Olivia won first honor of her class and Joseph the second. He was graduated June 1911. After a year and a half at Fisk University, Nashville, Tenn., Florence Olivia wrote us that Joseph had tuberculosis and must leave school. He returned home and was put under a doctor. The 16th of the following December, Florence Olivia returned from Fisk with tuberculosis, and one year from that day she died. It was grieving over his sister's death that discovered to Joseph his poetic talent. He died February 3rd, 1919, leaving his published poems,—*The Band of Gideon* and two other unpublished works—one of poems and one of one-act plays."

Joseph S. Cotter, Sr.

RAIN MUSIC

On the dusty earth-drum
Beats the falling rain;
Now a whispered murmur,
Now a louder strain.

Slender, silvery drumsticks,
  On an ancient drum,
Beat the mellow music
  Bidding life to come.

Chords of earth awakened,
  Notes of greening spring,
Rise and fall triumphant
  Over every thing.

Slender, silvery drumsticks
  Beat the long tattoo—
God, the Great Musician,
  Calling life anew.

SUPPLICATION

I AM so tired and weary,
  So tired of the endless fight,
So weary of waiting the dawn
  And finding endless night.

That I ask but rest and quiet—
  Rest for the days that are gone,
And quiet for the little space
  That I must journey on.

AN APRIL DAY

On such a day as this I think,
  On such a day as this,
When earth and sky and nature's whole
  Are clad in April's bliss;
And balmy zephyrs gently waft
  Upon your cheek a kiss;
Sufficient is it just to live
  On such a day as this.

THE DESERTER

I know not why or whence he came
  Or how he chanced to go;
I only know he brought me love
  And going, left me woe.

I do not ask that he turn back,
  Nor seek where he may rove;
For where woe rules can never be
  The dwelling place of love.

For love went out the door of hope,
  And on and on has fled;
Caring no more to dwell within
  The house where faith is dead.

AND WHAT SHALL YOU SAY?

BROTHER, come!
And let us go unto our God.
And when we stand before Him
I shall say—
"Lord, I do not hate,
I am hated.
I scourge no one,
I am scourged.
I covet no lands,
My lands are coveted.
I mock no peoples,
My people are mocked."
And, brother, what shall you say?

THE BAND OF GIDEON

THE band of Gideon roam the sky,
The howling wind is their war-cry,
The thunder's role is their trump's peal,
And the lightning's flash their vengeful steel.
 Each black cloud
 Is a fiery steed.
 And they cry aloud
 With each strong deed,
"The sword of the Lord and Gideon."

And men below rear temples high
And mock their God with reasons why,
And live in arrogance, sin and shame,
And rape their souls for the world's good name.
   Each black cloud
   Is a fiery steed.
   And they cry aloud
   With each strong deed,
"The sword of the Lord and Gideon."

The band of Gideon roam the sky,
And view the earth with baleful eye;
In holy wrath they scourge the land
With earth-quake, storm and burning brand.
   Each black cloud
   Is a fiery steed.
   And they cry aloud
   With each strong deed,
"The sword of the Lord and Gideon."

The lightnings flash and the thunders roll,
And "Lord have mercy on my soul,"
Cry men as they fall on the stricken sod,
In agony searching for their God.
   Each black cloud
   Is a fiery steed.
   And they cry aloud
   With each strong deed,
"The sword of the Lord and Gideon."

And men repent and then forget
That heavenly wrath they ever met,
The band of Gideon yet will come
And strike their tongues of blasphemy dumb.
  Each black cloud
  Is a fiery steed.
  And they cry aloud
  With each strong deed,
"The sword of the Lord and Gideon."

BLANCHE TAYLOR DICKINSON

I WAS born on a farm near Franklin, Kentucky, April
15, 1896, and received my education variously . . . public
schools, Bowling Green Academy, Simmon's University
and Summer schools.

No degree. Taught for several years in my native
state. I am a lover of music and divide my time between
the typewriter and piano. First published in *Franklin
Favorite,* later, *Louisville Leader, Chicago Defender,
Pittsburgh Courier, Crisis, Opportunity* and *Wayfarer.* My
favorite poets are Countee Cullen, Georgia Douglas John-
son and Edna St. Vincent Millay; my favorite past-time,
walking along a crowded street. I have a hunch that I
shall become a short story writer and my favorite exertion
is trying to perfect my "technique."

At present I am living in Sewickley, Penna.

THE WALLS OF JERICHO

JERICHO is on the inside
Of the things the world likes best;
"We want in," the dark ones cried,
"We will love it as the rest."

"Let me learn," the dark ones say.
They have learned that Faith must do
More than meditate and pray
That a boulder may fall through
Making one large man size entrance
Into wondrous Jericho.
They have learned: forget the distance,
Count no steps, nor stop to blow.

Jericho still has her high wall,
Futile barrier of Power. . . .
Echoed with the dark ones' footfall
Marching around her every hour;
Knowledge strapped down like a knapsack
Not cumbersome, and money
Not too much to strain the back. . . .
Dark ones seeking milk and honey.

Over in the city staring
Up at us along the wall
Are the fat ones, trembling, swearing
There is no room there for us all!

But there've been too many rounds
Made to give the trip up here.
Shout for joy . . . hear how it sounds. . . .
The very walls echo with cheer!

POEM

Ah, I know what happiness is. . . . !
It is a timid little fawn
Creeping softly up to me
For one caress, then gone
Before I'm through with it . . .
Away, like dark from dawn!
Well I know what happiness is . . . !
It is the break of day that wears
A shining dew decked diadem . . .
An aftermath of tears.
Fawn and dawn, emblems of joy . . .
I've played with them for years,
And always they will slip away
Into the brush of another day.

REVELATION

1

She walked along the crowded street
Forgetting all but that she

Was walking as the other girls
And dressed as carefully.

The windows of the stores were frilled
To lure femininity,
To empty little pocketbooks
And assuage queen vanity.

And so my walker liked a dress
Of silver and of gold,
Draped on a bisque mannequin
So blond and slim and bold.

She took the precious metal home
And waved her soft black hair;
Powder, rouge and lipstick made
Her very neat and fair.

She slipped the dress on carefully,
Her vain dream fell away. . . .
The mirror showed a brownskin girl
She hadn't seen all day!

2

"You have classic features,
Something like Cleopatra.
Eyes like whirlpools
And as dangerous. . . .
Weeping willow eyelashes

Shade the mighty depth
Of your eyes.   Your lips
Are danger signals
Which a fool like me
Will not regard. . . .
But go dashing past them
To gain a kiss . . . or Death."
            That is what he said to me,
I filled with a sweet and vain regret
That Beauty, the stranger, and I had met.
His praise was heat to drink me dry.
So I found a stream, and with a sigh
I stooped to drink . . . ah, to see
The cruel water reflecting me!
Dark-eyed, thick-lipped, harsh, short hair . . .
But Lucifer saw himself, too, fair.

THAT HILL

It crawled away from 'neath my feet
And left me standing there;
A little at a time, went up
An atmospheric stair.

I couldn't go for watching it,
To see where it would stop;
A tree sprang out and waved to me
When it had reached the top.

The tree kept nodding friendly like,
Beckoning me to follow;
And I went crawling up and up,
Like it did from the hollow.

Then I saw why the thing would go
A-soaring from the dell—
'Twas nearing Heaven every bound,
And fleeing fast from Hell!

TO AN ICICLE

CHILLED into a serenity
As rigid as your pose
You linger trustingly,
But a gutter waits for you.
Your elegance does not secure
You favors with the sun.
He is not one to pity fragileness.
He thinks all cheeks should burn
And feel how tears can run.

FOUR WALLS

FOUR great walls have hemmed me in.
Four strong, high walls:
Right and wrong,
Shall and shan't.

The mighty pillars tremble when
My conscience palls
And sings its song—
I can, I can't.

If for a moment Samson's strength
Were given me I'd shove
Them away from where I stand;
Free, I know I'd love
To ramble soul and all,
And never dread to strike a wall.

Again, I wonder would that be
Such a happy state for me . . .
The going, being, doing, sham—
And never knowing where I am.
I might not love freedom at all;
My tired wings might crave a wall—
Four walls to rise and pen me in
This conscious world with guarded men.

FRANK HORNE

BORN in New York City, August 18, 1899, I have lived
all but about six years in Brooklyn. I studied at the Col-
lege of the City of New York, and was guilty there of my
first sonnet; but am ever so much more proud of my varsity
letters won on the track—once ran a "10 flat" hundred and
a 51 sec. quarter. Went to the Northern Illinois College
of Ophthalmology—took degree "Doctor of Optometry."
Have practiced in Chicago and New York. At present

writing, am doing some teaching and publicity work at the Fort Valley High and Industrial School, Georgia, while recovering from a mean illness. Have had a hankering to write as long as I can remember, but Charles Johnson, Editor of *Opportunity* and a certain Gwendolyn Bennett are responsible for my trying it openly. My "published works" are limited to the indulgence of *Opportunity, The Crisis,* and *Braithwaite's Anthology.* It is the perversity of my nature to crave the ability to write good prose, and yet my attempts at poetry are the only things to which any notice is given."

ON SEEING TWO BROWN BOYS IN A CATHOLIC CHURCH

IT IS fitting that you be here
Little brown boys
With Christ-like eyes
And curling hair.

Look you on yon crucifix
Where He hangs nailed and pierced
With head hung low
And eyes a'blind with blood that drips
From a thorny crown . . .
Look you well,
You shall know this thing.

Judas' kiss will burn your cheek
And you shall be denied
By your Peter—

And Gethsemane . . .
You shall know full well
Gethsemane . . .

You, too, will suffer under Pontius Pilate
And feel the rugged cut of rough hewn cross
Upon your surging shoulder—
They will spit in your face
And laugh . . .
They will nail you up twixt thieves
And gamble for your little garments.

And in this you will exceed God
For on this earth
You shall know Hell—

O little brown boys
With Christ-like eyes
And curling hair
It is fitting that you be here.

TO A PERSISTENT PHANTOM

I BURIED you deeper last night
You with your tears
And your tangled hair
You with your lips
That kissed so fair
I buried you deeper last night.

I buried you deeper last night
With fuller breasts
And stronger arms
With softer lips
And newer charms
I buried you deeper last night.

Deeper . . . . . . aye, deeper
And again tonight
Till that gay spirit
That once was you
Will tear its soul
In climbing through . . .
Deeper . . . . . . aye, deeper
I buried you deeper last night.

LETTERS FOUND NEAR A SUICIDE

To all of you

My little stone
Sinks quickly
Into the bosom of this deep, dark pool
Of oblivion . . .
I have troubled its breast but little
Yet those far shores
That knew me not
Will feel the fleeting, furtive kiss
Of my tiny concentric ripples . . .

To Lewellyn

You have borne full well
The burden of my friendship—
I have drunk deep
At your crystal pool,
And in return
I have polluted its waters
With the bile of my hatred.
I have flooded your soul
With tortuous thoughts,
I have played Iscariot
To your Pythias . . .

To Mother

I came
In the blinding sweep
Of ecstatic pain,
I go
In the throbbing pulse
Of aching space—
In the eons between
I piled upon you
Pain on pain
Ache on ache
And yet as I go
I shall know
That you will grieve
And want me back . . .

To B——

You have freed me—
In opening wide the doors
Of flesh
You have freed me
Of the binding leash.
I have climbed the heights
Of white disaster
My body screaming
In the silver crash of passion . . .
Before you gave yourself
To him
I had chained myself
For you.
But when at last
You lowered your proud flag
In surrender complete
You gave me too, as hostage—
And I have wept my joy
At the dawn-tipped shrine
Of many breasts.

To Jean

When you poured your love
Like molten flame
Into the throbbing mold
Of her pulsing veins
Leaving her blood a river of fire
And her arteries channels of light,
I hated you . . .

Hated with that primal hate
That has its wells
In the flesh of me
And the flesh of you
And the flesh of her
I hated you—
Hated with envy
Your mastery of her being . . .
With one fleshy gesture
You pricked the iridescent bubble
Of my dreams
And so to make
Your conquest more sweet
I tell you now
That I hated you.

To Catalina

Love thy piano, Oh girl,
It will give you back
Note for note
The harmonies of your soul.
It will sing back to you
The high songs of your heart.
It will give
As well as take. . . .

To Mariette

I sought consolation
In the sorrow of your eyes.
You sought reguerdon

In the crying of my heart . . .
We found that shattered dreamers
Can be bitter hosts. . . .

To ——

You call it
Death of the Spirit
And I call it Life . . .
The vigor of vibration,
The muffled knocks,
The silver sheen of passion's flood,
The ecstasy of pain . . .
You call it
Death of the Spirit
And I call it Life.

To Telie

You have made my voice
A rippling laugh
But my heart
A crying thing . . .
'Tis better thus:
A fleeting kiss
And then,
The dark . . .

To "Chick"

Oh Achilles of the moleskins
And the gridiron
Do not wonder

Nor doubt that this is I
That lies so calmly here—
This is the same exultant beast
That so joyously
Ran the ball with you
In those far flung days of abandon.
You remember how recklessly
We revelled in the heat and the dust
And the swirl of conflict?
You remember they called us
The Terrible Two?
And you remember
After we had battered our heads
And our bodies
Against the stonewall of their defense,—
You remember the signal I would call
And how you would look at me
In faith and admiration
And say "Let's go," . . .
How the lines would clash
And strain,
And how I would slip through
Fighting and squirming
Over the line
To victory.
You remember, Chick? . . .
When you gaze at me here
Let that same light
Of faith and admiration
Shine in your eyes

For I have battered the stark stonewall
Before me . . .
I have kept faith with you
And now
I have called my signal,
Found my opening
And slipped through
Fighting and squirming
Over the line
To victory. . . .

To Wanda

To you, so far away
So cold and aloof,
To you, who knew me so well,
This is my last Grand Gesture
This is my last Great Effect
And as I go winging
Through the black doors of eternity
Is that thin sound I hear
Your applause? . . .

NIGGER

A Chant for Children

LITTLE Black boy
Chased down the street—
"Nigger, nigger never die

Black face an' shiney eye,
Nigger . . . nigger . . . nigger . . ."

Hannibal . . . Hannibal
Bangin' thru the Alps
Licked the proud Romans,
Ran home with their scalps—
"Nigger . . . nigger . . . nigger . . ."

Othello . . . black man
Mighty in war
Listened to Iago
Called his wife a whore—
"Nigger . . . nigger . . . nigger . . ."

Crispus . . . Attucks
Bullets in his chest
Red blood of freedom
Runnin' down his vest
"Nigger . . . nigger . . . nigger . . ."

Toussant . . . Toussant
Made the French flee
Fought like a demon
Set his people free—
"Nigger . . . nigger . . . nigger . . ."

Jesus . . . Jesus
Son of the Lord
—Spit in his face

    —Nail him on a board
    "Nigger . . . nigger . . . nigger . . ."

Little Black boy
Runs down the street—
"Nigger, nigger never die
Black face an' shiney eye,
Nigger . . . nigger . . . nigger . . ."

LEWIS ALEXANDER

LEWIS ALEXANDER was born July 4, 1900, at Washington, D. C. He was educated in the public schools of Washington and at Howard University where he was a member of the Howard Players. He has also studied at the University of Pennsylvania. He was a member of the Ethiopian Art Theatre for the season 1922-1923 playing in *Salome* and *The Comedy of Errors* on Broadway. As the result of a recent tour of North and South Carolina he edited in May 1927 the Negro Number of the *Carolina Magazine*. He has been writing poetry since 1917, specializing in Japanese forms. Two Little Theatre groups in Washington, The Ira Aldridge Players of the Grover Cleveland School and the Randall Community Center Players have been under his direction.

NEGRO WOMAN

THE sky hangs heavy tonight
Like the hair of a Negro woman.
The scars of the moon are curved

Like the wrinkles on the brow of a Negro woman.

The stars twinkle tonight
Like the glaze in a Negro woman's eyes,
Drinking the tears set flowing by an aging hurt
Gnawing at her heart.

The earth trembles tonight
Like the quiver of a Negro woman's eye-lids cupping
    tears.

AFRICA

THOU art not dead, although the spoiler's hand
Lies heavy as death upon thee; though the wrath
Of its accursed might is in thy path
And has usurped thy children of their land;
Though yet the scourges of a monstrous band
Roam on thy ruined fields, thy trampled lanes,
Thy ravaged homes and desolated fanes;
Thou art not dead, but sleeping,—Motherland.

A mighty country, valorous and free,
Thou shalt outlive this terror and this pain;
Shall call thy scattered children back to thee,
Strong with the memory of their brothers slain;
And rise from out thy charnel house to be
Thine own immortal, brilliant self again!

TRANSFORMATION

I ʀᴇᴛᴜʀɴ the bitterness,
   Which you gave to me;
When I wanted loveliness
   Tantalant and free.

I return the bitterness
   It is washed by tears;
Now it is a loveliness
   Garnished through the years.

I return it loveliness,
   Having made it so;
For I wore the bitterness
   From it long ago.

THE DARK BROTHER

"Lo, I am black but I am comely too,
   Black as the night, black as the deep dark caves.
I am the scion of a race of slaves
Who helped to build a nation strong that you
And I may stand within the world's full view,
Fearless and firm as dreadnoughts on rough waves;
Holding a banner high whose floating braves
The opposition of the tried untrue.

Casting an eye of love upon my face,
Seeing a newer light within my eyes,

A rarer beauty in your brother race
Will merge upon your visioning fullwise.
Though I am black my heart through love is pure,
And you through love my blackness shall endure!"

TANKA I—VIII

I

COULD I but retrace
The winding stairs fate built me.
They fell from my feet.
Now I stand on the high round.
Down beneath height above depth—

II

Through the eyes of life
I looked in at my own heart:
A long furrowed field
Grown cement waiting for seed
Baking in desolation.

III

Drink in moods of joy!
Why should the sky be lonely?
Neither sun nor moon—
How my heart is shy of night
Like Autumn's leaf brown pendants.

IV

Cold against the sky
The blue jays cried at dawning.
The larks where are they?
Heavily upon the air
My ears tuned in to listen.

V

So this is the reed?
The very pipes for singing—
Life plays me new songs.
Wistfully from out the dawn
The crows broke across the sky!

VI

And now Spring has come
Blossoming up my garden.
I alone unchanged.
Moving in my house of Autumn.
One leaf alone saves a tree.

VII

By the pool of life
Willows are drooping tonight
I can see no stars.
What dances in the water?
O my clouds dripping with tears.

VIII

Could I hear your voice
O but this silence is sweet
Words mar all beauty.
Turn then into your own heart
And pluck the roots from the soil—

JAPANESE HOKKU

O APPLE blossoms
Give me your words of silence,
Yes, your charming speech.

. . . .

If you would know me,
Do not regard this display;
Mingle with my speech.

. . . .

Why sit like the sphinx,
Watching the caravan pass?
Join in the parade.

. . . .

What if the wind blows?
What if the leaves are scattered,
Now that they are dead?

. . . .

While trimming the plants
I saw some flowers drooping.
I am a flower.

This is but my robe,
His Majesty gave to me.
Garments will decay.

. . . .

On the flowering twig,
Lo! the robin is singing.
It must be spring.

. . . .

Looking up the hill
The road was long before me.
This road is longer.

. . . .

Death is not cruel
From what I have seen of life;
Nothing else remains.

. . . .

Life is history.
Turn not away from the book.
Write on every page!

. . . .

If you had not sung
Then what would I imitate,
Happy nightingale?

. . . .

Sitting by the pool,
I looked in and saw my face.
O that I were blind!

DAY AND NIGHT

THE day is a Negro
   Yelling out of breath.
The night is a Negro
   Laughing up to death.

The day is a jazz band
   Blasting loud and wild.
The night is a jazz band
   Moaning Blues songs, child.

The day is the sunshine
   Undressed in the street.
The night is the sunshine
   Dressed from head to feet.

I am like a rainbow
   Arched across the way.
Yes, I am a rainbow
   Being night nor day.

STERLING A. BROWN

I WAS born in Washington, D. C., the first of May,
1901. I received primary and secondary education in the
Public Schools of that city, and on a farm near Laurel,
Md.; entered Williams College in 1918, was elected to
Phi Beta Kappa in 1921, graduated in 1922; and received
my Master of Arts Degree at Harvard in 1923. Since that

time I have been seeking a more liberal education teaching school. I have been inflicted on unsuspecting, helpless students; teaching diverse things at Manassas Summer School in Virginia, Rhetoric and Literature at Virginia Seminary and College, Lynchburg, Va., and Literature at Lincoln University, Jefferson City, Mo.

From early years I have *lisped in numbers* but the numbers seem improper fractions. I have always been interested in people, particularly and generally, and in books. The list runs from Homer to Housman.

Except for an essay on Roland Hayes submitted to an *Opportunity* contest, and occasional poems and reviews, I have published nothing of the voluminous works cluttering my desk.

ODYSSEY OF BIG BOY

LEMME be wid Casey Jones,
   Lemme be wid Stagolee,
Lemme be wid such like men
   When Death takes hol' on me,
     When Death takes hol' on me. . . .

Done skinned as a boy in Kentucky hills,
   Druv steel dere as a man,
Done stripped tobacco in Virginia fiels'
   Alongst de River Dan,
     Alongst de River Dan;

Done mined de coal in West Virginia
   Liked dat job jes' fine

Till a load o' slate curved roun' my head
  Won't work in no mo' mine,
    Won't work in no mo' mine;

Done shocked de corn in Marylan,
  In Georgia done cut cane,
Done planted rice in South Caline,
  But won't do dat again
    Do dat no mo' again.

Been roustabout in Memphis,
  Dockhand in Baltimore,
Done smashed up freight on Norfolk wharves
  A fust class stevedore,
    A fust class stevedore. . . .

Done slung hash yonder in de North
  On de ole Fall River Line
Done busted suds in li'l New Yawk
  Which ain't no work o' mine—
    Lawd, ain't no work o' mine;

Done worked and loafed on such like jobs
  Seen what dey is to see
Done had my time with a pint on my hip
  An' a sweet gal on my knee
    Sweet mommer on my knee:

Had stovepipe blonde in Macon
  Yaller gal in Marylan

In Richmond had a choklit brown
  Called me huh monkey man—
  Huh big fool monkey man

Had two fair browns in Arkansaw
  And three in Tennessee
Had Creole gal in New Orleans
  Sho Gawd did two time me—
    Lawd two time, fo' time me—

But best gal what I evah had
  Done put it over dem
A gal in Southwest Washington
  At Four'n half and M—
    Four'n half and M. . . .

Done took my livin' as it came
  Done grabbed my joy, done risked my life
Train done caught me on de trestle
  Man done caught me wid his wife
    His doggone purty wife . . .

I done had my women,
  I done had my fun
Cain't do much complainin'
  When my jag is done,
    Lawd, Lawd, my jag is done.

An' all dat Big Boy axes
  When time comes fo' to go

Lemme be wid John Henry, steel drivin' man
Lemme be wid ole Jazzbo;
　　Lemme be wid ole Jazzbo. . . .

MAUMEE RUTH

MIGHT as well bury her
　　And bury her deep,
Might as well put her
　　Where she can sleep.

Might as well lay her
　　Out in her shiny black;
And for the love of God
　　Not wish her back.

Maum Sal may miss her
　　Maum Sal, she only
With no one now to scoff
　　Sal may be lonely. . . .

Nobody else there is
　　Who will be caring
How rocky was the road
　　For her wayfaring;

Nobody be heeding in
　　Cabin, or town
That she is lying here
　　In her best gown.

Boy that she suckled
How should he know
Hiding in city holes
Sniffing the 'snow'?

And how should the news
Pierce Harlem's din
To reach her baby gal,
Sodden with gin?

To cut her withered heart
They cannot come again,
Preach her the lies about
Jordan and then

Might as well drop her
Deep in the ground
Might as well pray for her
That she sleep sound. . . .

LONG GONE

I LAKS yo' kin' of lovin'
Ain't never caught you wrong
But it jes ain' nachal
Fo' to stay here long;

It jes ain' nachal
Fo' a railroad man

With a itch fo' travellin'
  He cain't understan'. . . .

I looks at de rails
  An' I looks at de ties,
An I hears an ole freight
  Puffin' up de rise,

An' at nights on my pallet
  When all is still
I listens fo' de empties
  Bumpin' up de hill;

When I oughta be quiet
  I is got a itch
Fo' to hear de whistle blow
  Fo' de crossin', or de switch

An' I knows de time's a nearin'
  When I got to ride
Though its homelike and happy
  At yo' side.

You is done all you could do
  To make me stay
Tain't no fault of yours I'se leavin'—
  I'se jes dataway.

I is got to see some people
  I ain' never seen

Gotta highball thu some country
Whah I never been. . . .

I don't know which way I'm travellin'—
Far or near,
All I knows fo' certain is
I cain't stay here

Ain't no call at all, sweet woman
Fo' to carry on,—
Jes my name and jes my habit
To be Long Gone. . . .

TO A CERTAIN LADY, IN HER GARDEN

(A. S.)

LADY, my lady, come from out the garden,
Clayfingered, dirtysmocked, and in my time
I too shall learn the quietness of Arden,
Knowledge so long a stranger to my rhyme.

What were more fitting than your springtime task?
Here, close engirdled by your vines and flowers
Surely there is no other grace to ask,
No better cloister from the bickering hours.

A step beyond, the dingy streets begin
With all their farce, and silly tragedy—

But here, unmindful of the futile din
You grow your flowers, far wiser certainly,

You and your garden sum the same to me,
A sense of strange and momentary pleasure,
And beauty snatched—oh, fragmentarily
Perhaps, yet who can boast of other seizure?

Oh, you have somehow robbed, I know not how
The secret of the loveliness of these
Whom you have served so long. Oh, shameless, now
You flaunt the winnings of your thieveries.

Thus, I exclaim against you, profiteer. . . .
For purpled evenings spent in pleasing toil,
Should you have gained so easily the dear
Capricious largesse of the miser soil?

Colorful living in a world grown dull,
Quiet sufficiency in weakling days,
Delicate happiness, more beautiful
For lighting up belittered, grimy ways—

Surely I think I shall remember this,
You in your old, rough dress, bedaubed with clay,
Your smudgy face parading happiness,
Life's puzzle solved. Perhaps, in turn, you may

One time, while clipping bushes, tending vines,
(Making your brave, sly mock at dastard days,)

Laugh gently at these trivial, truthful lines—
And that will be sufficient for my praise.

SALUTAMUS

(O Gentlemen the time of Life is short—Henry IV)

THE bitterness of days like these we know;
Much, much we know, yet cannot understand
What was our crime that such a searing brand
Not of our choosing, keeps us hated so.
Despair and disappointment only grow,
Whatever seeds are planted from our hand,
What though some roads wind through a gladsome
    land?
It is a gloomy path that we must go.

And yet we know relief will come some day
For these seared breasts; and lads as brave again
Will plant and find a fairer crop than ours.
It must be due our hearts, our minds, our powers;
These are the beacons to blaze out the way.
We must plunge onward; onward, gentlemen. . . .

CHALLENGE

I SAID, in drunken pride of youth and you
That mischief-making Time would never dare
Play his ill-humoured tricks upon us two,

Strange and defiant lovers that we were.
I said that even Death, Highwayman Death,
Could never master lovers such as we,
That even when his clutch had throttled breath,
My hymns would float in praise, undauntedly.

I did not think such words were bravado.
Oh, I think honestly we knew no fear,
Of Time or Death. We loved each other so.
And thus, with you believing me, I made
My prophecies, rebellious, unafraid. . . .
And that was foolish, wasn't it, my dear?

RETURN

I HAVE gone back in boyish wonderment
To things that I had foolishly put by. . . .
Have found an alien and unknown content
In seeing how some bits of cloud-filled sky
Are framed in bracken pools; through chuckling hours
Have watched the antic frogs, or curiously
Have numbered all the unnamed, vagrant flowers,
That fleck the unkempt meadows, lavishly.

Or where a headlong toppling stream has stayed
Its racing, lulled to quiet by the song
Bursting from out the thickleaved oaken shade,
There I have lain while hours sauntered past—
I have found peacefulness somewhere at last,
Have found a quiet needed for so long.

CLARISSA SCOTT DELANY

"I WAS born at Tuskegee Institute, Alabama, in the Twentieth Century, and spent my early years in what is known as the 'Black Belt.' This was followed by seven years in New England (1916-1923), three at Bradford Academy, and four at Wellesley College, where my southern blood became tinged with something of the austerity of that section. Three years of teaching in the Dunbar High School of Washington, D. C., convinced me that though the children were interesting, teaching was not my *metier*. In the fall of 1926 I was married. Since completing a study of Delinquency and Neglect among Negro children in New York City, my career has been that of a wife, and as careers go, that is an interesting and absorbing one."

JOY

Joy shakes me like the wind that lifts a sail,
Like the roistering wind
That laughs through stalwart pines.
It floods me like the sun
On rain-drenched trees
That flash with silver and green.

I abandon myself to joy—
I laugh—I sing.
Too long have I walked a desolate way,
Too long stumbled down a maze
Bewildered.

SOLACE

My window opens out into the trees
And in that small space
Of branches and of sky
I see the seasons pass
Behold the tender green
Give way to darker heavier leaves.
The glory of the autumn comes
When steeped in mellow sunlight
The fragile, golden leaves
Against a clear blue sky
Linger in the magic of the afternoon
And then reluctantly break off
And filter down to pave
A street with gold.
Then bare, gray branches
Lift themselves against the
Cold December sky
Sometimes weaving a web
Across the rose and dusk of late sunset
Sometimes against a frail new moon
And one bright star riding
A sky of that dark, living blue
Which comes before the heaviness
Of night descends, or the stars
Have powdered the heavens.
Winds beat against these trees;
The cold, but gentle rain of spring

Touches them lightly
The summer torrents strive
To lash them into a fury
And seek to break them—
But they stand.
My life is fevered
And a restlessness at times
An agony—again a vague
And baffling discontent
Possesses me.
I am thankful for my bit of sky
And trees, and for the shifting
Pageant of the seasons.
Such beauty lays upon the heart
A quiet.
Such eternal change and permanence
Take meaning from all turmoil
And leave serenity
Which knows no pain.

INTERIM

THE night was made for rest and sleep,
For winds that softly sigh;
It was not made for grief and tears;
So then why do I cry?

The wind that blows through leafy trees
Is soft and warm and sweet;

For me the night is a gracious cloak
To hide my soul's defeat.

Just one dark hour of shaken depths,
Of bitter black despair—
Another day will find me brave,
And not afraid to dare.

THE MASK

So detached and cool she is
No motion e'er betrays
The secret life within her soul,
The anguish of her days.

She seems to look upon the world
With cold ironic eyes,
To spurn emotion's fevered sway,
To scoff at tears and sighs.

But once a woman with a child
Passed by her on the street,
And once she heard from casual lips
A man's name, bitter-sweet.

Such baffled yearning in her eyes,
Such pain upon her face!
I turned aside until the mask
Was slipped once more in place.

LANGSTON HUGHES

LANGSTON HUGHES was born in Joplin, Missouri, on the
first of February, 1902. His mother was a school teacher,
his father a lawyer. During most of his childhood he
lived with his grandmother in Lawrence, Kansas, where
he went to school. This old lady, Mary Sampson Patter-
son Leary Langston, was the last surviving widow of
John Brown's Raid, her first husband having been one
of the five colored men to die so gloriously at Harper's
Ferry. She had then married Charles Langston, brother
of the Negro senator, John M. Langston, and in the seven-
ties they came to Kansas where the mother of the poet
was born.

When Langston Hughes was thirteen this grandmother
died and the boy went to live with his mother in Lincoln,
Illinois. A year later they moved to Cleveland where he
attended and was graduated from the Central High School.
Then followed fifteen months in Mexico where his father
had been located for some years. Here the young man
learned Spanish, taught English, and attended bull-fights.
Here, too, he wrote "The Negro Speaks of Rivers," his
first poem to be published in the magazines.

In 1921 he went to New York for a year at Columbia
University. A break with his father followed and he
secured work for the summer on a truck farm on Staten
Island. Then for almost two years he travelled as a
member of the crew of freight steamers voyaging to the
West Coast of Africa and Northern Europe. In Febru-
ary, 1924, he went to Paris. When he arrived he had seven
dollars in his pockets; so he soon found a job as doorman
in a Montmartre cabaret. Later he became second cook
and pan-cake maker at the Grand Duc, a Negro night
club where Buddy Gilmore sometimes played and Florence
sang. That summer he went to Italy, and September

found him stranded in Genoa. He worked his way back to New York on a tramp steamer, painting and scrubbing decks.

A year in Washington followed where he worked in the office of the Association for the Study of Negro Life and History, and later as a bus boy at the Wardman Park Hotel. There Vachel Lindsay read some of his poems and he was discovered by the newspapers. Then his first book, *The Weary Blues,* appeared. He has now resumed his formal education at Lincoln University in Pennsylvania, which he says is a place of beauty and the ideal college for a poet. His second book of poems, *Fine Clothes for the Jew,* is a study in racial rhythms.

Lincoln University
April 13, 1927

I, TOO[1]

I, TOO, sing America.

I am the darker brother.
They send me to eat in the kitchen
When company comes,
But I laugh,
And eat well,
And grow strong.

Tomorrow,
I'll sit at the table

[1] By permission of and special arrangement with Alfred A. Knopf, Inc., authorized publishers.

When company comes.
Nobody'll dare
Say to me,
"Eat in the kitchen,"
Then.

Besides,
They'll see how beautiful I am
And be ashamed,—

I, too, am America.

PRAYER[1]

I ASK you this:
Which way to go?
I ask you this:
Which sin to bear?
Which crown to put
Upon my hair?
I do not know,
Lord God,
I do not know.

[1] By permission of and special arrangement with Alfred A. Knopf, Inc., authorized publishers.

SONG FOR A DARK GIRL[1]

WAY down South in Dixie
　(Break the heart of me)
They hung my black young lover
　To a cross roads tree.

Way down South in Dixie
　(Bruised body high in air)
I asked the white Lord Jesus
　What was the use of prayer.

Way down South in Dixie
　(Break the heart of me)
Love is a naked shadow
　On a gnarled and naked tree.

HOMESICK BLUES[2]

DE RAILROAD bridge's
A sad song in de air.
De railroad bridge's
A sad song in de air.
Ever time de trains pass
I wants to go somewhere.

I went down to de station.
Ma heart was in ma mouth.
Went down to de station.
Heart was in ma mouth.
Lookin' for a box car
To roll me to de South.

Homesick blues, Lawd,
'S a terrible thing to have.
Homesick blues is
A terrible thing to have.
To keep from cryin'
I opens ma mouth an' laughs.

FANTASY IN PURPLE[1]

BEAT the drums of tragedy for me.
Beat the drums of tragedy and death.
And let the choir sing a stormy song
To drown the rattle of my dying breath.

Beat the drums of tragedy for me,
And let the white violins whir thin and slow,
But blow one blaring trumpet note of sun
To go with me
        to the darkness
            where I go.

DREAM VARIATION[1]

To FLING my arms wide
In some place of the sun,
To whirl and to dance
Till the white day is done.
Then rest at cool evening
Beneath a tall tree
While night comes on gently,
    Dark like me,—
That is my dream!

To fling my arms wide
In the face of the sun,
Dance! whirl! whirl!
Till the quick day is done.
Rest at pale evening. . . .
A tall, slim tree. . . . .
Night coming tenderly
    Black like me.

THE NEGRO SPEAKS OF RIVERS[2]

I'VE known rivers:
I've known rivers ancient as the world and older than
the flow of human blood in human veins.

My soul has grown deep like the rivers.

I bathed in the Euphrates when dawns were young.
I built my hut near the Congo and it lulled me to sleep.
I looked upon the Nile and raised the pyramids above it.
I heard the singing of the Mississippi when Abe Lincoln
      went down to New Orleans, and I've seen its muddy
      bosom turn all golden in the sunset.

I've known rivers:
Ancient, dusky rivers.

My soul has grown deep like the rivers.

POEM[1]

THE night is beautiful,
So the faces of my people.

The stars are beautiful,
So the eyes of my people.

Beautiful, also, is the sun.
Beautiful, also, are the souls of my people.

[1] By permission of and special arrangement with Alfred A. Knopf, Inc., authorized publishers.

SUICIDE'S NOTE[1]

THE calm,
Cool face of the river
Asked me for a kiss.

MOTHER TO SON[2]

WELL, son, I'll tell you:
Life for me ain't been no crystal stair.
It's had tacks in it,
And splinters,
And boards torn up,
And places with no carpet on the floor—
Bare.
But all the time
I's been a-climbin' on,
And reachin' landin's,
And turnin' corners,
And sometimes goin' in the dark
Where there ain't been no light.
So boy, don't you turn back.
Don't you set down on the steps
'Cause you finds it's kinder hard.
Don't you fall now—
For I's still goin', honey,

---

[1] By permission of and special arrangement with Alfred A. Knopf, Inc., authorized publishers.
[2] By permission of and special arrangement with Alfred A. Knopf, Inc., authorized publishers.

I's still climbin',
And life for me ain't been no crystal stair.

A HOUSE IN TAOS

Rain

THUNDER of the Rain God:
    And we three
    Smitten by beauty.

Thunder of the Rain God:
    And we three
    Weary, weary.

Thunder of the Rain God:
    And you, she and I
    Waiting for nothingness.

Do you understand the stillness
    Of this house in Taos
Under the thunder of the Rain God?

Sun

That there should be a barren garden
About this house in Taos
Is not so strange,
But that there should be three barren hearts
In this one house in Taos,—
Who carries ugly things to show the sun?

Moon

Did you ask for the beaten brass of the moon?
We can buy lovely things with money,
You, she and I,
Yet you seek,
As though you could keep,
This unbought loveliness of moon.

Wind

Touch our bodies, wind.
Our bodies are separate, individual things.
Touch our bodies, wind,
But blow quickly
Through the red, white, yellow skins
Of our bodies
To the terrible snarl,
Not mine,
Not yours,
Not hers,
But all one snarl of souls.
Blow quickly, wind,
Before we run back into the windlessness,—
With our bodies,—
Into the windlessness
Of our house in Taos.

GWENDOLYN B. BENNETT

GWENDOLYN B. BENNETT was born in Giddings, Texas,
on July 8th, 1902. Her father was a lawyer and her mother

was a school teacher.   She received her elementary train-
ing in the Public Schools of Washington, D. C., and Har-
risburg, Pa.   She was graduated from the Girls' High
School in Brooklyn, New York, during January, 1921.
While she was in attendance there she was a member of
the Felter Literary Society and the Girls' High School
Dramatic Society, being the first Negro girl to have been
elected to either of these societies.   In an open contest
she was awarded the first prize for a poster bearing the
slogan *Fresh Air Prevents Tuberculosis.*

She matriculated in the Fine Arts Department of
Teachers' College, Columbia University, where she re-
mained for two years.   She then entered the Normal Art
Course at Pratt Institute, Brooklyn, New York.   She was
the author of her class play each of the two years she
was there.   In her Junior Year she played the leading
part in the play which she had herself written.   She was
graduated from Pratt Institute June 1924.

She then became a member of the Howard University
Faculty in Fine Arts as Instructor in Design, Water-color
and Crafts.   During the Christmas holidays of the school
year 1924-25 Miss Bennett was awarded the Thousand
Dollar Foreign Scholarship by the Alpha Sigma Chapter
of the Delta Sigma Theta Sorority at its Annual Conven-
tion held in New York City.

She sailed for Cherbourg, France on June fifteenth,
1925.   While in Paris she studied at the Académie Julian,
The Académie Coloraossi and the École de Pantheon.
Through the influence of Konrad Bercovici she was thrown
in contact with the artist, Frans Masereel, one of France's
best known modern painters.   M. and Mme. Masereel
offered Miss Bennett the hospitality of their home and
together with their circle of friends did much to encourage
her in her work while in Paris.   She returned to America
during June 1926.

For the summer of 1926 she was employed at the *Op-*

portunity magazine where she acted in the capacity of Assistant to the Editor. September 1926 she returned to Howard University where she resumed her classroom work after a year's leave of absence.

QUATRAINS

1

Brushes and paints are all I have
To speak the music in my soul—
While silently there laughs at me
A copper jar beside a pale green bowl.

2

How strange that grass should sing—
Grass is so still a thing. . . .
And strange the swift surprise of snow
So soft it falls and slow.

SECRET

I shall make a song like your hair . . .
Gold-woven with shadows green-tinged,
And I shall play with my song
As my fingers might play with your hair.
Deep in my heart
I shall play with my song of you,

Gently. . . .
I shall laugh
At its sensitive lustre . . .
I shall wrap my song in a blanket,
Blue like your eyes are blue
With tiny shots of silver.
I shall wrap it caressingly,
Tenderly. . . .
I shall sing a lullaby
To the song I have made
Of your hair and eyes . . .
And you will never know
That deep in my heart
I shelter a song of you
Secretly. . . .

ADVICE

You were a sophist,
Pale and quite remote,
As you bade me
Write poems—
Brown poems
Of dark words
And prehistoric rhythms . . .
Your pallor stifled my poesy
But I remembered a tapestry
That I would some day weave
Of dim purples and fine reds

And blues
Like night and death—
The keen precision of your words
Wove a silver thread
Through the dusk softness
Of my dream-stuff. . . .

TO A DARK GIRL

I LOVE you for your brownness
And the rounded darkness of your breast.
I love you for the breaking sadness in your voice
And shadows where your wayward eye-lids rest.

Something of old forgotten queens
Lurks in the lithe abandon of your walk
And something of the shackled slave
Sobs in the rhythm of your talk.

Oh, little brown girl, born for sorrow's mate,
Keep all you have of queenliness,
Forgetting that you once were slave,
And let your full lips laugh at Fate!

YOUR SONGS

WHEN first you sang a song to me
With laughter shining from your eyes,

You trolled your music liltingly
With cadences of glad surprise.

In after years I heard you croon
In measures delicately slow
Of trees turned silver by the moon
And nocturnes sprites and lovers know.

And now I cannot hear you sing,
But love still holds your melody
For silence is a sounding thing
To one who listens hungrily.

FANTASY

I SAILED in my dreams to the Land of Night
Where you were the dusk-eyed queen,
And there in the pallor of moon-veiled light
The loveliest things were seen . . .

A slim-necked peacock sauntered there
In a garden of lavender hues,
And you were strange with your purple hair
As you sat in your amethyst chair
With your feet in your hyacinth shoes.

Oh, the moon gave a bluish light
Through the trees in the land of dreams and night.
I stood behind a bush of yellow-green
And whistled a song to the dark-haired queen . . .

LINES WRITTEN AT THE GRAVE
OF ALEXANDER DUMAS

CEMETERIES are places for departed souls
And bones interred,
Or hearts with shattered loves.
A woman with lips made warm for laughter
Would find grey stones and roving spirits
Too chill for living, moving pulses . . .
And thou, great spirit, wouldst shiver in thy granite
    shroud
Should idle mirth or empty talk
Disturb thy tranquil sleeping.

A cemetery is a place for shattered loves
And broken hearts. . . .
Bowed before the crystal chalice of thy soul,
I find the multi-colored fragrance of thy mind
Has lost itself in Death's transparency.

Oh, stir the lucid waters of thy sleep
And coin for me a tale
Of happy loves and gems and joyous limbs
And hearts where love is sweet!

A cemetery is a place for broken hearts
And silent thought . . .
And silence never moves,
Nor speaks nor sings.

HATRED

I SHALL hate you
Like a dart of singing steel
Shot through still air
At even-tide.
Or solemnly
As pines are sober
When they stand etched
Against the sky.
Hating you shall be a game
Played with cool hands
And slim fingers.
Your heart will yearn
For the lonely splendor
Of the pine tree;
While rekindled fires
In my eyes
Shall wound you like swift arrows.
Memory will lay its hands
Upon your breast
And you will understand
My hatred.

SONNET

1

HE came in silvern armour, trimmed with black—
A lover come from legends long ago—

With silver spurs and silken plumes a-blow,
And flashing sword caught fast and buckled back
In a carven sheath of Tamarack.
He came with footsteps beautifully slow,
And spoke in voice meticulously low.
He came and Romance followed in his track. . . .

I did not ask his name—I thought him Love;
I did not care to see his hidden face.
All life seemed born in my intaken breath;
All thought seemed flown like some forgotten dove.
He bent to kiss and raised his visor's lace . . .
All eager-lipped I kissed the mouth of Death.

SONNET

2

Some things are very dear to me—
Such things as flowers bathed by rain
Or patterns traced upon the sea
Or crocuses where snow has lain . . .
The iridescence of a gem,
The moon's cool opalescent light,
Azaleas and the scent of them,
And honeysuckles in the night.
And many sounds are also dear—
Like winds that sing among the trees
Or crickets calling from the weir
Or Negroes humming melodies.

But dearer far than all surmise
Are sudden tear-drops in your eyes.

ARNA BONTEMPS

ARNA BONTEMPS explains that he was just tall enough to see above window sills when the first trolley car came down Lee Street in Alexandria, La. His mother, Marie Pembroke, had been born in this same town but his father had come out of Marksville, a smaller town of that state. Though exceedingly young and very frail, Marie Pembroke had taught school until her marriage, while her husband, Paul Bontemps, was a brick mason, the son and grandson of brick masons.

With Arna Bontemps in his third year and a second child, a girl, just past one, the family left the South for San Francisco. However, they stopped in Los Angeles to visit relatives and have never moved further. Here the boy's mother died some nine years later and here his father is still living. Here also he received his early education in a rather irregular attendance of a number of schools. He went through the schools rapidly enough and in spite of being out several years received a college degree in his twentieth year.

In the year following that he lost his illusions with reference to a musical career and returned to an original intention to eat bread by the sweat of teaching school. It is to be remembered that he went to college first with the purpose of taking a medical course but it took him only a day or two to decide better.

He lives in New York City and is now twenty-four and married.

THE RETURN

I

ONCE more, listening to the wind and rain,
Once more, you and I, and above the hurting sound
Of these comes back the throbbing of remembered rain,
Treasured rain falling on dark ground.
Once more, huddling birds upon the leaves
And summer trembling on a withered vine.
And once more, returning out of pain,
The friendly ghost that was your love and mine.

II

Darkness brings the jungle to our room:
The throb of rain is the throb of muffled drums.
Darkness hangs our room with pendulums
Of vine and in the gathering gloom
Our walls recede into a denseness of
Surrounding trees.   This is a night of love
Retained from those lost nights our fathers slept
In huts; this is a night that must not die.
Let us keep the dance of rain our fathers kept
And tread our dreams beneath the jungle sky.

III

And now the downpour ceases.
Let us go back once more upon the glimmering leaves

And as the throbbing of the drums increases
Shake the grass and dripping boughs of trees.
A dry wind stirs the palm; the old tree grieves.

Time has charged the years: the old days have returned.

Let us dance by metal waters burned
With gold of moon, let us dance
With naked feet beneath the young spice trees.
What was that light, that radiance
On your face?—something I saw when first
You passed beneath the jungle tapestries?

A moment we pause to quench our thirst
Kneeling at the water's edge, the gleam
Upon your face is plain: you have wanted this.
Let us go back and search the tangled dream
And as the muffled drum-beats throb and miss
Remember again how early darkness comes
To dreams and silence to the drums.

IV

Let us go back into the dusk again,
Slow and sad-like following the track
Of blowing leaves and cool white rain
Into the old gray dream, let us go back.
Our walls close about us we lie and listen
To the noise of the street, the storm and the driven
    birds.

A question shapes your lips, your eyes glisten
Retaining tears, but there are no more words.

A BLACK MAN TALKS OF REAPING

I HAVE sown beside all waters in my day.
I planted deep, within my heart the fear
That wind or fowl would take the grain away.
I planted safe against this stark, lean year.

I scattered seed enough to plant the land
In rows from Canada to Mexico
But for my reaping only what the hand
Can hold at once is all that I can show.

Yet what I sowed and what the orchard yields
My brother's sons are gathering stalk and root,
Small wonder then my children glean in fields
They have not sown, and feed on bitter fruit.

TO A YOUNG GIRL LEAVING THE HILL COUNTRY

THE hills are wroth; the stones have scored you bitterly
Because you looked upon the naked sun
Oblivious of them, because you did not see
The trees you touched or mountains that you walked
   upon.

But there will come a day of darkness in the land,
A day wherein remembered sun alone comes through
To mark the hills; then perhaps you'll understand
Just how it was you drew from them and they from you.

For there will be a bent old woman in that day
Who, feeling something of this country in her bones,
Will leave her house tapping with a stick, who will (they
    say)
Come back to seek the girl she was in these familiar
    stones.

NOCTURNE AT BETHESDA

I THOUGHT I saw an angel flying low,
I thought I saw the flicker of a wing
Above the mulberry trees; but not again.
Bethesda sleeps. This ancient pool that healed
A host of bearded Jews does not awake.
This pool that once the angels troubled does not move.
No angel stirs it now, no Saviour comes
With healing in His hands to raise the sick
And bid the lame man leap upon the ground.

The golden days are gone. Why do we wait
So long upon the marble steps, blood
Falling from our open wounds? and why
Do our black faces search the empty sky?

Is there something we have forgotten? some precious
   thing
We have lost, wandering in strange lands?

There was a day, I remember now,
I beat my breast and cried, "Wash me God,
Wash me with a wave of wind upon
The barley; O quiet One, draw near, draw near!
Walk upon the hills with lovely feet
And in the waterfall stand and speak.

"Dip white hands in the lily pool and mourn
Upon the harps still hanging in the trees
Near Babylon along the river's edge,
But oh, remember me, I pray, before
The summer goes and rose leaves lose their red."

The old terror takes my heart, the fear
Of quiet waters and of faint twilights.
There will be better days when I am gone
And healing pools where I cannot be healed.
Fragrant stars will gleam forever and ever
Above the place where I lie desolate.

Yet I hope, still I long to live.
And if there can be returning after death
I shall come back. But it will not be here;
If you want me you must search for me
Beneath the palms of Africa. Or if
I am not there then you may call to me

Across the shining dunes, perhaps I shall
Be following a desert caravan.

I may pass through centuries of death
With quiet eyes, but I'll remember still
A jungle tree with burning scarlet birds.
There is something I have forgotten, some precious
    thing.
I shall be seeking ornaments of ivory,
I shall be dying for a jungle fruit.

       You do not hear, Bethesda.
O still green water in a stagnant pool!
Love abandoned you and me alike.
There was a day you held a rich full moon
Upon your heart and listened to the words
Of men now dead and saw the angels fly.
There is a simple story on your face;
Years have wrinkled you. I know, Bethesda!
You are sad. It is the same with me.

LENGTH OF MOON

    THEN the golden hour
    Will tick its last
    And the flame will go down in the flower.

    A briefer length of moon
    Will mark the sea-line and the yellow dune.

Then we may think of this, yet
There will be something forgotten
And something we should forget.

It will be like all things we know:
The stone will fail; a rose is sure to go.

It will be quiet then and we may stay
As long at the picket gate
But there will be less to say.

LANCELOT

THE fruit of the orchard is over-ripe, Elaine,
And leaves are crisping on the garden wall.
Leaves on the garden path are wet and rain
Drips from the low shrubs with a steady fall.

It is long, so long since I was here, Elaine,
Moles have gnawed the rose tree at its root;
You did not think that I would come again,
Least of all in the day of falling fruit.

GETHSEMANE

ALL that night I walked alone and wept.
I tore a rose and dropped it on the ground.
My heart was lead; all that night I kept
Listening to hear a dreadful sound.

A tree bent down and dew dripped from its hair.
The earth was warm; dawn came solemnly.
I stretched full-length upon the grass and there
I said your name but silence answered me.

A TREE DESIGN

A TREE is more than a shadow
Blurred against the sky,
More than ink spilled on the fringe
Of white clouds floating by.
A tree is more than an April design
Or a blighted winter bough
Where love and music used to be.
A tree is something in me,
Very still and lonely now.

BLIGHT

I HAVE seen a lovely thing
Stark before a whip of weather:
The tree that was so wistful after spring
Beating barren twigs together.

The birds that came there one by one,
The sensuous leaves that used to sway
And whisper there at night, all are gone,
Each has vanished in its way.

And this whip is on my heart;
There is no sound that it allows,
No little song that I may start
But I hear the beating of dead boughs.

THE DAY-BREAKERS

WE are not come to wage a strife
    With swords upon this hill.
It is not wise to waste the life
    Against a stubborn will.
Yet would we die as some have done:
Beating a way for the rising sun.

CLOSE YOUR EYES!

Go THROUGH the gates with closed eyes.
Stand erect and let your black face front the west.
Drop the axe and leave the timber where it lies;
A woodman on the hill must have his rest.

Go where leaves are lying brown and wet.
Forget her warm arms and her breast who mothered
        you,
And every face you ever loved forget.
Close your eyes; walk bravely through.

GOD GIVE TO MEN

God give the yellow man
An easy breeze at blossom time.
Grant his eager, slanting eyes to cover
Every land and dream
Of afterwhile.

Give blue-eyed men their swivel chairs
To whirl in tall buildings.
Allow them many ships at sea,
And on land, soldiers
And policemen.

For black man, God,
No need to bother more
But only fill afresh his meed
Of laughter,
His cup of tears.

God suffer little men
The taste of soul's desire.

HOMING

Sweet timber land
Where soft winds blow
The high green tree

And fan away the fog!
Ah fragrant stream
Where thirsty creatures go
And strong black men
Hew the heavy log!

Oh broken house
Crumbling there alone,
Wanting me!
Oh silent tree
Must I always be
A wild bird
Riding the wind
And screaming bitterly?

GOLGOTHA IS A MOUNTAIN

GOLGOTHA is a mountain, a purple mound
Almost out of sight.
One night they hanged two thieves there,
And another man.
Some women wept heavily that night;
Their tears are flowing still.   They have made a river;
Once it covered me.
Then the people went away and left Golgotha
Deserted.
Oh, I've seen many mountains:
Pale purple mountains melting in the evening mists and
    blurring on the borders of the sky.

I climbed old Shasta and chilled my hands in its summer
    snows.
I rested in the shadow of Popocatepetl and it whispered
    to me of daring prowess.
I looked upon the Pyrenees and felt the zest of warm
    exotic nights.
I slept at the foot of Fujiyama and dreamed of legend
    and of death.
And I've seen other mountains rising from the wistful
    moors like the breasts of a slender maiden.
Who knows the mystery of mountains!
Some of them are awful, others are just lonely.

*   *   *

Italy has its Rome and California has San Francisco,
All covered with mountains.
Some think these mountains grew
Like ant hills
Or sand dunes.
That might be so—
I wonder what started them all!
Babylon is a mountain
And so is Ninevah,
With grass growing on them;
Palaces and hanging gardens started them.
I wonder what is under the hills
In Mexico
And Japan!
There are mountains in Africa too.

Treasure is buried there:
Gold and precious stones
And moulded glory.
Lush grass is growing there
Sinking before the wind.
Black men are bowing.
Naked in that grass
Digging with their fingers.
I am one of them:
Those mountains should be ours.
It would be great
To touch the pieces of glory with our hands.
These mute unhappy hills,
Bowed down with broken backs,
Speak often one to another:
"A day is as a year," they cry,
"And a thousand years as one day."
We watched the caravan
That bore our queen to the courts of Solomon;
And when the first slave traders came
We bowed our heads.
"Oh, Brothers, it is not long!
Dust shall yet devour the stones
But we shall be here when they are gone."
Mountains are rising all around me.
Some are so small they are not seen;
Others are large.
All of them get big in time and people forget
What started them at first.

Oh the world is covered with mountains!
Beneath each one there is something buried:
Some pile of wreckage that started it there.
Mountains are lonely and some are awful.

* * *

One day I will crumble.
They'll cover my heap with dirt and that will make a
    mountain.
I think it will be Golgotha.

ALBERT RICE

I AM a native of our Capital City, born in the Mauve
Decade (1903). My schooling has been in the Washing-
ton grammar and high schools. It was while a student at
Dunbar High School that I felt a restless urge to write
something other than dull formal paragraphs in English.
I made several attempts at verse but found them so poor
that I hastily put such ideas behind me.

After leaving high school I entered the government serv-
ice in Washington, but my radical views could not be-
come reconciled to the conservative bourgeoise ideals
around me; so I left the government service and journeyed
to New York in the winter of 1926. Here I served an
apprenticeship in literary vagabondage with the bizarre
and eccentric young vagabond poet of High Harlem,
Richard Bruce. It was here that I felt inspired to write
"The Black Madonna." I was one evening at vespers
down at St. Mary's the Virgin, and while lost in con-
templation before Our Lady, I thought of a Madonna of
swart skin, a Madonna of dark mien.

Despite my radicalism I am religious. I admire the socialist form of government, and my favorite poet is Claude McKay. And some day I hope to flee the shores of this exquisite hell. My temperament is Latin. I abhor all things Anglo-Saxon. I'd rather live in the squalor of Mulberry Street, N. Y. (Little Italy) than at Irvington-on-the-Hudson. I love bull fights and dislike baseball games. I like dancing and dislike prayer meetings. I love New York because it is crowded and noisy and an outpost of Europe. Of my home here in Washington I have not much to offer. I like Washington because it has such a large share of Babbitts, both white and black. And I like it because Georgia Douglas Johnson lives there and on Saturday nights has an assembly of likable and civilized people, and because it was from this Saturday night circle that Jean Toomer, Richard Bruce, and Richard Goodwin, the artist, went forth to fame and infamy.

THE BLACK MADONNA

NOT as the white nations
    know thee
        O Mother!

But swarthy of cheek
    and full-lipped as the
        child races are.

Yet thou art she,
    the Immaculate Maid,
        and none other,

Crowned in the stable
at Bethlehem,
hailed of the star.

See where they come,
thy people,
so humbly appealing,

From the ancient lands
where the olden faiths
had birth.

Tired dusky hands
uplifted for thy
healing.

Pity them, Mother,
the untaught
of earth.

COUNTEE CULLEN

BORN in New York City, May 30, 1903, and reared in the conservative atmosphere of a Methodist parsonage, Countee Cullen's chief problem has been that of reconciling a Christian upbringing with a pagan inclination. His life so far has not convinced him that the problem is insoluble. Educated in the elementary and high schools of New York City, with an A.B. degree and a Phi Beta Kappa Key from New York University, an M.A. from Harvard, arrantly opposed to any form of enforced racial segregation, he finds it a matter of growing regret that no part of his academic education has been drawn from a racial school. As a poet he is a rank conservative, loving the measured line and the skillful rhyme; but not blind to the virtues of those poets who will not be circumscribed; and he is thankful indeed for the knowledge that should he ever desire to go adventuring, the world is rife with paths to choose from. He has said, perhaps with a reiteration sickening to some of his friends, that he wishes any merit that may be in his work to flow from it solely as the expression of a poet—with no racial consideration to bolster it up. He is still of the same thought. At present he is employed as Assistant Editor of *Opportunity, A Journal of Negro Life*.

His published works are *Color, The Ballad of the Brown Girl,* and *Copper Sun.*

LINES TO OUR ELDERS

You too listless to examine
If in pestilence or famine
Death lurk least, a hungry gamin

Gnawing on you like a beaver
On a root, while you trifle
Time away nodding in the sun,
Careless how the shadows crawl
Surely up your crumbling wall,
Heedless of the Thief's footfall,
Death's, whose nimble fingers rifle
Your heartbeats one by weary one,—
Here's the difference in our dying:
You go dawdling, we go flying.
Here's a thought flung out to plague you:
Ours the pleasure if we'd liever
Burn completely with the fever
Than go ambling with the ague.

I HAVE A RENDEZVOUS WITH LIFE

(With apologies to the memory of Alan Seeger)

I HAVE a rendezvous with Life
In days I hope will come
Ere youth has sped and strength of mind,
Ere voices sweet grown dumb;
I have a rendezvous with Life
When Spring's first heralds hum.
It may be I shall greet her soon,
Shall riot at her behest;

It may be I shall seek in vain
The peace of her downy breast;
Yet I would keep this rendezvous,
And deem all hardships sweet,
If at the end of the long white way,
There Life and I shall meet.
Sure some will cry it better far
To crown their days in sleep,
Than face the wind, the road, and rain,
To heed the falling deep;
Though wet, nor blow, nor space I fear,
Yet fear I deeply, too,
Lest Death shall greet and claim me ere
I keep Life's rendezvous.

PROTEST

I LONG not now, a little while at least,
For that serene interminable hour
When I shall leave this barmecidal feast,
With poppy for my everlasting flower.
I long not now for that dim cubicle
Of earth to which my lease will not expire,
Where he who comes a tenant there may dwell
Without a thought of famine, flood, or fire.

Surely that house has quiet to bestow:
Still tongue, spent pulse, heart pumped of its last throb,
The fingers tense and tranquil in a row,

The throat unwelled with any sigh or sob.
But time to live, to love, bear pain and smile,
Oh, we are given such a little while!

YET DO I MARVEL

I DOUBT not God is good, well-meaning, kind,
And did he stoop to quibble could tell why
The little buried mole continues blind,
Why flesh that mirrors him must some day die,
Make plain the reason tortured Tantalus
Is baited with the fickle fruit, declare
If merely brute caprice dooms Sisyphus
To struggle up a never-ending stair.

Inscrutable His ways are and immune
To catechism by a mind too strewn
With petty cares to slightly understand
What awful brain compels His awful hand;
Yet do I marvel at this curious thing:
To make a poet black, and bid him sing!

TO LOVERS OF EARTH: FAIR WARNING

GIVE over to high things the fervent thought
You waste on Earth; let down the righteous bar

Against a wayward peace too dearly bought
Upon this pale and passion-frozen star.
Sweethearts and friends, are they not loyal? Far
More fickle, false, perverse, far more unkind,
Is Earth to those who give her heart and mind.

And you whose lusty youth her snares intrigue,
Who glory in her seas, swear by her clouds,
With Age, man's foe, Earth ever is in league.
Time resurrects her even while he crowds
Your bloom to dust, and lengthens out your shrouds
A day's length or a year's. She will be young
When your last cracked and quivering note is sung.

She will remain the Earth, sufficient still
Though you are gone, and with you that rare loss
That vanishes with your bewildered will;
And there shall flame no red, indignant cross
For you, no quick white scar of wrath emboss
The sky, no blood drip from a wounded moon,
And not a single star chime out of tune.

FROM THE DARK TOWER

WE SHALL not always plant while others reap
The golden increment of bursting fruit,
Not always countenance, abject and mute,
That lesser men should hold their brothers cheap;
Not everlastingly while others sleep

Shall we beguile their limbs with mellow flute,
Not always bend to some more subtle brute;
We were not made eternally to weep.

The night whose sable breast relieves the stark
White stars is no less lovely, being dark;
And there are buds that cannot bloom at all
In light, but crumple, piteous, and fall;
So in the dark we hide the heart that bleeds,
And wait, and tend our agonizing seeds.

TO JOHN KEATS, POET, AT SPRINGTIME

I CANNOT hold my peace, John Keats;
There never was a spring like this;
It is an echo, that repeats
My last year's song and next year's bliss.
I know, in spite of all men say
Of Beauty, you have felt her most.
Yea, even in your grave her way
Is laid. Poor, troubled, lyric ghost,
Spring never was so fair and dear
As Beauty makes her seem this year.

I cannot hold my peace, John Keats;
I am as helpless in the toil
Of Spring as any lamb that bleats
To feel the solid earth recoil

Beneath his puny legs.   Spring beats
Her tocsin call to those who love her,
And lo! the dogwood petals cover
Her breast with drifts of snow, and sleek
White gulls fly screaming to her, and hover
About her shoulders, and kiss her cheek,
While white and purple lilacs muster
A strength that bears them to a cluster
Of color and odor; for her sake
All things that slept are now awake.

And you and I, shall we lie still,
John Keats, while Beauty summons us?
Somehow I feel your sensitive will
Is pulsing up some tremulous
Sap road of a maple tree, whose leaves
Grow music as they grow, since your
Wild voice is in them, a harp that grieves
For life that opens death's dark door.
Though dust, your fingers still can push
The Vision Splendid to a birth,
Though now they work as grass in the hush
Of the night on the broad sweet page of the earth.

"John Keats is dead," they say, but I
Who hear your full insistent cry
In bud and blossom, leaf and tree,
Know John Keats still writes poetry.
And while my head is earthward bowed
To read new life sprung from your shroud,

Folks seeing me must think it strange
That merely spring should so derange
My mind. They do not know that you,
John Keats, keep revel with me, too.

FOUR EPITAPHS

1

For My Grandmother

THIS lovely flower fell to seed;
Work gently sun and rain;
She held it as her dying creed
That she would grow again.

2

For John Keats, Apostle of Beauty

Not writ in water nor in mist,
Sweet lyric throat, thy name.
Thy singing lips that cold death kissed
Have seared his own with flame.

3

For Paul Laurence Dunbar

Born of the sorrowful of heart
Mirth was a crown upon his head;

Pride kept his twisted lips apart
In jest, to hide a heart that bled.

4

For a Lady I Know

She even thinks that up in heaven
   Her class lies late and snores,
While poor black cherubs rise at seven
   To do celestial chores.

INCIDENT

ONCE riding in old Baltimore,
   Heart-filled, head-filled with glee,
I saw a Baltimorean
   Keep looking straight at me.

Now I was eight and very small,
   And he was no whit bigger,
And so I smiled, but he poked out
   His tongue and called me, "Nigger."

I saw the whole of Baltimore
   From May until December:
Of all the things that happened there
   That's all that I remember.

DONALD JEFFREY HAYES

DONALD JEFFREY HAYES was born November 16, 1904, in Raleigh, N. C. At the age of five his parents brought him to Atlantic City, N. J., where he attended the public schools through the freshman year of High School. In 1913 he moved with his family to Pleasantville, N. J., where in his sophomore year of High School he was awarded, after a near student strike, court action and the dismissal of a member of the faculty—the highest debating honors. Following this unpleasantness, he went to Chicago where he studied privately the forms of poetry while completing his High School work. He graduated in 1926 from Englewood an honor student, and distinguished, as it were, as "The poet of Englewood" and "The Bronze God" as his fellow students dubbed him.

He is at present planning a volume of his verse and studying the voice, planning to make his career in the concert field.

INSCRIPTION

HE WROTE upon his heart
As on the door of some dark ancient house:
Who once lived here has long been dead
As dead as moss-grown stone
Only a ghost inhabits here
One that would be alone
Only a ghost inhabits here
A ghost without desire
Who sits before a shadowed hearth
And warms to a spectral fire. . . . . . .

AUF WIEDERSEHEN

I SHALL come this way again
 On some distant morrow
When the red and golden leaves
 Have fallen on my sorrow . . . !

I shall come this way again
 When this day is rotten
In the grave of yesterdays
 And this hour forgotten. . . . !

I shall come this way again
 Before the lamp light dies
To comfort you and dry the tear
 Of penance from your eyes. . . . !

NIGHT

 NIGHT like purple flakes of snow
 Falls with ease
 Catching on the roofs of houses
 In the tops of trees
 Down upon the distant grass
 And the distant flower
 It will drift into this room
 In an hour. . . . .

CONFESSION

SHE kneeled before me begging
  That I should with a prayer
Give her absolution
  (How golden was her hair!)

She begged an absolution
  While the moments fled
She thought my tears were pity
  (My soul her lips were red!)

She begged of me forgiveness
  God you understand
(For pale and soft and slender
  Was her dainty hand!)

She begged that I should pray You
  That her Soul might rest
But I could not pray O Master
  (Ivory was her breast!)

NOCTURNE

SOFTLY blow lightly
O twilight breeze
Scarcely bend slightly
O silver trees:

Night glides slowly down hill . . down stream
Bringing a myriad star-twinkling dream. . . . .
Softly blow lightly
O twilight breeze
Scarcely bend slightly
O silver trees:
Night will spill sleep in your day weary eye
While a soft yellow moon steals down the sky. . . .
Softly blow
Scarcely bend
So . . . . !
Lullaby. . . . . . .

AFTER ALL

After all and after all
When the song is sung
And swallowed up in silence
It were more real unsung. . . .

After all and after all
When the lips have stirred
Such a little of the thought
Is transmuted in the word. . . . . .

Suffer not my ears with hearing
Suffer not your thoughts with speech.
Let us feel into our meaning
And thus know the all of each.

JONATHAN HENDERSON BROOKS

I was born on a farm twelve miles southwest of Lexington, Mississippi, in 1904. When I was eleven years old our family was disunited by divorce. My three sisters and only brother went with father while I chose to become my mother's "little ploughman." We worked around on "half shares" in the community of my birth until I was fourteen, and then my mother, who had managed somehow to save enough money to keep me in school for four months, sent me to Jackson College. It was here that I received my first material recognition for writing when I was awarded the first prize in a local contest for my first story, entitled "The Bible In The Cotton Field." Mother's plan was to send me back to Jackson College again the following year, but the white landlord took her entire crop of four bales to cover the land rent of my uncle with whom we had gone to live in Humphreys County that year.

My formal education has been interrupted more than once by periods of farming and teaching. I moved up my years and taught two five-months sessions in Humphreys County before I finished my high school work. In the fall of 1923 I matriculated at Lincoln University, Missouri, and graduated from its high school department in June 1925 with salutatory honors. Lincoln was very kind to me during those two years—the happiest I have known in all my life. It gave me work enough to cover my expenses while attending there, twice chose me the president of my class, and bestowed upon me each of the three first prizes it offers in the high school department, besides electing me class poet and giving me a host of staunch friends.

I am now pursuing my college work at Tougaloo Col-

lege and am part time pastor of the second Baptist Church
of Kosciusko, Mississippi.

THE RESURRECTION

His friends went off and left Him dead
In Joseph's subterranean bed,
Embalmed with myrrh and sweet aloes,
And wrapped in snow-white burial clothes.

Then shrewd men came and set a seal
Upon His grave, lest thieves should steal
His lifeless form away, and claim
For Him an undeserving fame.

"There is no use," the soldiers said,
"Of standing sentries by the dead."
Wherefore, they drew their cloaks around
Themselves, and fell upon the ground,
And slept like dead men, all night through,
In the pale moonlight and chilling dew.

A muffled whiff of sudden breath
Ruffled the passive air of death.

He woke, and raised Himself in bed;
    Recalled how He was crucified;
Touched both hands' fingers to His head,
    And lightly felt His fresh-healed side.

Then with a deep, triumphant sigh,
He coolly put His grave-clothes by—
Folded the sweet, white winding sheet,
  The toweling, the linen bands,
  The napkin, all with careful hands—
And left the borrowed chamber neat.

His steps were like the breaking day:
  So soft across the watch He stole,
  He did not wake a single soul,
Nor spill one dewdrop by the way.

Now Calvary was loveliness:
  Lilies that flowered thereupon
Pulled off the white moon's pallid dress,
  And put the morning's vesture on.

"Why seek the living among the dead?
He is not here," the angel said.

The early winds took up the words,
And bore them to the lilting birds,
The leafing trees, and everything
That breathed the living breath of spring.

THE LAST QUARTER MOON OF THE DYING YEAR

THE last quarter moon of the dying year,
Pendant behind a naked cottonwood tree
On a frosty, dawning morning
With the back of her silver head
Turned to the waking sun.
Quiet like the waters
Of Galilee
After the Lord had bid them
"Peace, be still."
O silent beauty, indescribable!

Dead, do they say?
Would God that I shall seem
So beautiful in death.

PAEAN

ACROSS the dewy lawn she treads
    Before the sun awakes
While lush, green grasses bow their heads
    To kiss the tracks she makes.

The violets, in clusters, stand
    And stare her beauty through,
And seem so happy in her hand,
    They know not what to do.

She must have come whence zephyrs blow,
From sprites' or angels' lands;
Her heart is meet for God to know—
Oh, heaven is where she stands!

GLADYS MAY CASELY HAYFORD

"I was born at Axim on the African Gold Coast in 1904 on the 11th of May to singularly cultured and intellectual parents, my mother being one of the daughters of Judge Smith, the first Judge of the Excomission Court of Sierra Leone, and my father being one of the three pioneer lawyers of the Gold Coast.

I am a Fanti, of the Fanti tribe which spreads from Axim right down the Gold Coast, to Acera, and is subdivided into groups speaking different dialects. It is said that the Acera branch, at one time, wandered away from the main body and eventually arrived also at the sea coast, speaking another tongue, but retaining the same customs.

I spent five years in England, three of which were spent in school. I went to Penrohs College, Colwyn Bay in Wales, and on my return home became a school teacher in The Girls Vocational School, Sierra Leone.

By twenty, I had the firm conviction that I was meant to write for Africa. This was accentuated by the help which our boys and girls need so much and fired by the determination to show those who are prejudiced against colour, that we deny inferiority to them, spiritually, intellectually and morally; and to prove it.

I argued that the first thing to do, was to imbue our own people with the idea of their own beauty, superiority and individuality, with a love and admiration for our own country, which has been systematically suppressed. Con-

sequently I studied the beautiful points of Negro phys-
ique, texture of skin, beauty of hair, soft sweetness of
eyes, charm of curves, so that none should think it a
shame to be black, but rather a glorious adventure."

NATIVITY

WITHIN a native hut, ere stirred the dawn,
Unto the Pure One was an Infant born
Wrapped in blue lappah that his mother dyed.
Laid on his father's home-tanned deer-skin hide
The babe still slept by all things glorified.
Spirits of black bards burst their bonds and sang,
"Peace upon earth" until the heavens rang.
All the black babies who from earth had fled,
Peeped through the clouds, then gathered round His
    head.
Telling of things a baby needs to do,
When first he opens his eyes on wonders new;
Telling Him that to sleep was sweeter rest,
All comfort came from His black mother's breast.
Their gifts were of Love caught from the springing sod,
Whilst tears and laughter were the gifts of God.
Then all the wise men of the past stood forth
Filling the air East, West, and South and North;
And told him of the joys that wisdom brings
To mortals in their earthly wanderings.
The children of the past shook down each bough,
Wreathed Frangepani blossoms for His brow;
They put pink lilies in His mother's hand,

And heaped for both the first fruits of the land.
His father cut some palm fronds that the air
Be coaxed to zephyrs while He rested there.
Birds trilled their hallelujahs; and the dew
Trembled with laughter till the babe laughed too.
All the black women brought their love so wise,
And kissed their motherhood into his mother's eyes.

Note: lappah—a straight woven cloth tied round the waist to form a
      skirt.
      Frangepani—An African flower.

RAINY SEASON LOVE SONG

OUT of the tense awed darkness, my Frangepani comes;
Whilst the blades of Heaven flash round her, and the
      roll of thunder drums
My young heart leaps and dances, with exquisite joy
      and pain,
As storms within and storms without I meet my love in
      the rain.

"The rain is in love with you darling; it's kissing you
      everywhere,
Rain pattering over your small brown feet, rain in your
      curly hair;
Rain in the vale that your twin breasts make, as in
      delicate mounds they rise,
I hope there is rain in your heart, Frangepani, as rain
      half fills your eyes."

Into my hands she cometh, and the lightning of my
   desire
Flashes and leaps about her, more subtle than Heaven's
   fire;
"The lightning's in love with you darling; it is loving
   you so much,
That its warm electricity in you pulses wherever I may
   touch.
When I kiss your lips and your eyes, and your hands
   like twin flowers apart,
I know there is lightning, Frangepani, deep in the
   depths of your heart."

The thunder rumbles about us, and I feel its triumphant
   note
As your warm arms steal around me; and I kiss your
   dusky throat;
"The thunder's in love with you darling. It hides its
   power in your breast.
And I feel it stealing o'er me as I lie in your arms at
   rest.
I sometimes wonder, beloved, when I drink from life's
   proffered bowl,
Whether there's thunder hidden in the innermost parts
   of your soul."

Out of my arms she stealeth; and I am left alone with
   the night,
Void of all sounds save peace, the first faint glimmer
   of light.

Into the quiet, hushed stillness my Frangepani goes.
Is there peace within like the peace without?   Only the
darkness knows.

THE SERVING GIRL

THE calabash wherein she served my food,
Was smooth and polished as sandalwood:
Fish, as white as the foam of the sea,
Peppered, and golden fried for me.
She brought palm wine that carelessly slips
From the sleeping palm tree's honeyed lips.
But who can guess, or even surmise
The countless things she served with her eyes?

BABY COBINA

BROWN BABY COBINA, with his large black velvet eyes,
His little coos of ecstacies, his gurgling of surprise,
With brass bells on his ankles, that laugh where'er he
goes,
It's so rare for bells to tinkle, above brown dimpled
toes.

BROWN BABY COBINA is so precious that we fear
Something might come and steal him, when we grown-
ups are not near;

So we tied bells on his ankles, and kissed on them this
    charm—
"Bells, guard our Baby Cobina from all devils and all
    harm."

LUCY ARIEL WILLIAMS

LUCY ARIEL WILLIAMS was born in Mobile, Alabama,
March 3, 1905. Her parents, Dr. and Mrs. H. Roger
Williams surrounded her with the aesthetic and cultural
environment usually given the only daughters in profes-
sional homes in the South. Miss Williams is well known
as a modiste, poet and extremely talented pianist. Her
early training was acquired at Emerson Institute, Mobile,
Alabama. Later she was graduated from Talladega Col-
lege and Fisk University, after which she attended Ober-
lin Conservatory of Music, Oberlin, Ohio. Although a
first year student there, she received third year classifica-
tion, being the first member of her race to be so honored.
Her work has appeared in *Opportunity* and other journals.
Her poem "Northboun'" received first prize in the *Oppor-
tunity* contest for 1926.

NORTHBOUN'

O' DE wurl' ain't flat,
An' de wurl' ain't roun',
H'it's one long strip
Hangin' up an' down—
Jes' Souf an' Norf;
Jes' Norf an' Souf.

Talkin' 'bout sailin' 'round de wurl'—
Huh! I'd be so dizzy my head 'ud twurl.
If dis heah earf wuz jes' a ball
You no the people all 'ud fall.

O' de wurl' ain't flat,
An' de wurl' ain't roun',
H'it's one long strip
Hangin' up an' down—
Jes' Souf an' Norf;
Jes' Norf an' Souf.

Talkin' 'bout the City whut Saint John saw —
Chile you oughta go to Saginaw;
A nigger's chance is "finest kind,"
An' pretty gals ain't hard to find.

Huh! de wurl' ain't flat,
An' de wurl' ain't roun',
Jes' one long strip
Hangin' up an' down.
Since Norf is up,
An' Souf is down,
An' Hebben is up,
I'm upward boun'.

GEORGE LEONARD ALLEN

I was born in Lumberton, North Carolina, September 10, 1905. My parents, Professor and Mrs. D. P. Allen, were then in charge of Whitin Normal School, a thriving secondary school which was discontinued at my father's death some ten years ago.

My high school days were spent at Redstone Academy, located at Lumberton. I can think of nothing of interest to mention concerning this period, except that I was an omnivorous reader, and learned to love literature, and especially poetry, with a passionate intensity.

Four years of college at Johnson C. Smith University followed, during which time I studied a little, read a great deal, and dabbled in music and literature. Among other things, I experimented with the piano enough to become a fairly advanced performer.

It was during my stay at college that my longing to become a writer grew particularly ardent. A good many of my literary attempts saw the light in school and local periodicals, some bringing encouraging comment. In June of 1926, I was graduated, having been chosen as valedictorian for that year.

I feel it necessary to mention here that my college career was made possible mainly through the sacrifices of my noble and devoted mother.

In the past winter I was engaged in teaching at Kendall Institute in Sumter, S. C. During this time some of my work appeared in *Opportunity, American Life, The Southwestern Christian Advocate,* and *The Lyric West.*

This year one of my poems, "To Melody," was awarded the prize for the best sonnet in a state-wide contest conducted by the United Daughters of the Confederacy (North Carolina Division).

TO MELODY

I THINK that man hath made no beauteous thing
More lovely than a glorious melody
That soars aloft in splendor, full and free,
And graceful as a swallow on the wing!
A melody that seems to move, and sing,
And quiver, in its radiant ecstasy,
That bends and rises like a slender tree
Which sways before the gentle winds of Spring!

Ah, men will ever love thee, holy art!
For thou, of all the blessings God hath given,
Canst best revive and cheer the wounded heart
And nearest bring the weary soul to Heaven!
Of all God's precious gifts, it seems to me,
The choicest is the gift of melody.

PORTRAIT

HER eyes?   Dark pools of deepest shade,
    Like sylvan lakes that lie
In some sequestered forest glade
    Beneath a starry sky.

Her cheeks?   The ripened chestnut's hue,—
    Rich autumn's sun-kissed brown!
Caressed by sunbeams dancing through
    Red leaves that flutter down.

Her form? A slender pine that sways
 Before the murmuring breeze
In summer, when the south wind plays
 Soft music through the trees.

Herself? A laughing, joyous sprite
 Who smiles from dawn till dark,
As lovely as a summer night
 And carefree as a lark.

RICHARD BRUCE

I was born in Washington, D. C., on the second of July,
1906, and have never ceased to marvel at the fact. After
attending public school with very good marks (I was
thrashed if I did not lead my class), I attended Dunbar
High School of the same city. When I was thirteen my
father died, my greatest impression being the crowded
church and the vault. Mother left Washington for New
York where my brother and I joined her in a few months.
New York was an adventure and still is. A glorious
something torn from a novel. Even the first hard winter
with mother ill and my feet on the ground was just a part
of it. My gathering bits of fur to paste on newspaper to
cut out for inner soles for my shoes, the walking to work
to save carfare, and getting lunch as best I could, all
seemed romantic and highly colored. Weren't there the-
atres and lights, Broadway, Fifth Avenue . . . and lights?
Noise and bustle and high silk hats and flowers in pots
in the Bowery. Hobble cars creeping like caterpillars up
Broadway. Taxis and people and forty-second street.
Traffic towers and tall buildings. Wasn't this New York?
A year later I discovered Harlem. I was at that time

an art apprentice at seven fifty a week. But that was too little money. So I became in turn errand boy for ten dollars, bell hop in an all-womens' hotel for eleven fifty-five, eighteen with tips, secretary and confidence man for a modiste for twenty-five, ornamental iron-worker and designer for twenty-eight, and elevator operator for thirty. Then I had the mumps and despite the glamor of New York, I wanted to go, just go somewhere. So I went to Panama working my way. Then New York again and a costume design class. A visit home to D. C. where I met Langston Hughes. *Opportunity* accepted my first poem. Washington for eleven months then New York again. I arrived penniless and have remained so. Dilatory jobs, trips to New England, Florida, California and Canada, but always New York again. The few drawings and sketches made on these trips were either destroyed, lost, or given away en route. I began to write seriously and to paint just as seriously; I entered contests but never won. I am still penniless and happy and planning to go to Paris and Vienna by hook or crook.

SHADOW

SILHOUETTE
On the face of the moon
Am I.
A dark shadow in the light.
A silhouette am I
On the face of the moon
Lacking color
Or vivid brightness
But defined all the clearer

Because
I am dark,
Black on the face of the moon.
A shadow am I
Growing in the light,
Not understood as is the day,
But more easily seen
Because
I am a shadow in the light.

CAVALIER

SLAY fowl and beast; pluck clean the vine,
Prepare the feast and pearl the wine.
Bring on the best! Bring on the bard,
Bring on the rest. Let nought retard
Nor yet distress with putrid breath,
My new mistress, My Lady Death.

WARING CUNEY

WARING CUNEY was born in Washington, D. C., May 6,
1906. He received his education in the public schools of
that city and at Howard University. Later he attended
Lincoln University, and while there sang in the Glee Club
and the quartet. His work with these groups encouraged
him to study music and he is now studying voice at the
New England Conservatory of Music in Boston. His
first published poem was "No Images" which won first
award in the *Opportunity* contest of 1926. Since then he

has continued to write and his poems have appeared in *Opportunity,* Braithwaite's *Anthology, The Forum,* and *Palms.*

THE DEATH BED

ALL the time they were praying
He watched the shadow of a tree
Flicker on the wall.

There is no need of prayer,
He said,
No need at all.

The kin-folk thought it strange
That he should ask them from a dying bed.
But they left all in a row
And it seemed to ease him
To see them go.

There were some who kept on praying
In a room across the hall
And some who listened to the breeze
That made the shadows waver
On the wall.

He tried his nerve
On a song he knew
And made an empty note

That might have come,
From a bird's harsh throat.

And all the time it worried him
That they were in there praying
And all the time he wondered
What it was they could be saying.

A TRIVIALITY

Not to dance with her
Was such a trivial thing

There were girls more fair than she,—

To-day
Ten girls dressed in white.
Each had a white rose wreath.

They made a dead man's arch
And ten strong men
Carried a body through.

Not to dance with her
Was a trivial thing.

I THINK I SEE HIM THERE

I THINK I see Him there
With a stern dream on his face

I see Him there—

Wishing they would hurry
The last nail in place.

And I wonder, had I been there,
Would I have doubted too

Or would the dream have told me,
What this man speaks is true.

DUST

Dust,

Through which
Proud blood
Once flowed.

Dust,

Where a civilization
Flourished.

Dust,
The Valley of the Nile,
Dust,

You proud ones, proud of the skill
With which you play this game—Civilization;
Do not forget that it is a very old game.
Men used to play it on the banks
Of the Tigris and the Euphrates
When the world was a wilderness.

There is a circle around China
Where once a wall stood.
Carthage is a heap of ashes.
And Rome knew the pomp and glory
You know now.

The Coliseum tells a story
The Woolworth Building may repeat.

Dust,
Pharaohs and their armies sleep there.

Dust,
Shall it stir again?

Will Pharaohs rise and rule
And their armies march once more?

Civilization continually shifts
Upon the places of the earth.

NO IMAGES

SHE does not know
Her beauty,
She thinks her brown body
Has no glory.

If she could dance
Naked,
Under palm trees
And see her image in the river
She would know.

But there are no palm trees
On the street,
And dish water gives back no images.

THE RADICAL

MEN never know
What they are doing.
They always make a muddle
Of their affairs,
They always tie their affairs
Into a knot
They cannot untie.
Then I come in
Uninvited.

They do not ask me in;
I am the radical,
The bomb thrower,
I untie the knot
That they have made,
And they never thank me.

TRUE LOVE

HER love is true I know,
Much more true
Than angel's love;
For angels love in heaven
Where a thousand harps
Are playing.

She loves in a tenement
Where the only music
She hears
Is the cry of street car brakes
And the toot of automobile horns
And the drip of a kitchen spigot
All day.
Her love is true I know.

EDWARD S. SILVERA

I WAS born in Florida in the year 1906—moved to
Orange, N. J., at an early age—graduated from Orange

High School in 1924—am now a Junior at Lincoln University, Pennsylvania. Here I am a member of the varsity basket-ball and tennis teams and a member of Kappa Alpha Psi Fraternity.

I get a great deal of pleasure out of observing life and then writing about it just as I see it.

SOUTH STREET

(Philadelphia, Pa.)

South Street is not beautiful,
But the songs of people there
Hold the beauty of the jungle,
And the fervidness of prayer.

South Street has no mansions,
But the hands of South Street men
Built pyramids along the Nile
That Time has failed to rend.

South Street is America,
Breast of the foster mother
Where a thousand ill-kept children
Vie for suck, with one another.

JUNGLE TASTE

There is a coarseness
In the songs of black men

Coarse as the songs
Of the sea,
There is a weird strangeness
In the songs of black men
Which sounds not strange
To me.

There is beauty
In the faces of black women,
Jungle beauty
And mystery
Dark hidden beauty
In the faces of black women,
Which only black men
See.

HELENE JOHNSON

HELENE JOHNSON was born twenty years ago in Boston,
Mass., where she received her early education and attended
Boston University for a short time. A year ago she came
to New York to attend the Extension Division of Columbia
University. Her work has appeared in *Opportunity,
Vanity Fair* and several New York dailies; and has been
reprinted in *Palms, The Literary Digest,* and Braithwaite's
Anthology.

WHAT DO I CARE FOR MORNING

WHAT do I care for morning,
For a shivering aspen tree,
For sun flowers and sumac
Opening greedily?
What do I care for morning,
For the glare of the rising sun,
For a sparrow's noisy prating,
For another day begun?
Give me the beauty of evening,
The cool consummation of night,
And the moon like a love-sick lady,
Listless and wan and white.
Give me a little valley
Huddled beside a hill,
Like a monk in a monastery,
Safe and contented and still,
Give me the white road glistening,
A strand of the pale moon's hair,
And the tall hemlocks towering
Dark as the moon is fair.
Oh what do I care for morning,
Naked and newly born—
Night is here, yielding and tender—
What do I care for dawn!

SONNET TO A NEGRO IN HARLEM

You are disdainful and magnificent—
Your perfect body and your pompous gait,
Your dark eyes flashing solemnly with hate,
Small wonder that you are incompetent
To imitate those whom you so despise—
Your shoulders towering high above the throng,
Your head thrown back in rich, barbaric song,
Palm trees and mangoes stretched before your eyes.
Let others toil and sweat for labor's sake
And wring from grasping hands their meed of gold.
Why urge ahead your supercilious feet?
Scorn will efface each footprint that you make.
I love your laughter arrogant and bold.
You are too splendid for this city street!

SUMMER MATURES

Summer matures. Brilliant Scorpion
Appears. The Pelican's thick pouch
Hangs heavily with perch and slugs.
The brilliant-bellied newt flashes
Its crimson crest in the white water.
In the lush meadow, by the river,
The yellow-freckled toad laughs
With a toothless gurgle at the white-necked stork
Standing asleep on one red reedy leg.

And here Pan dreams of slim stalks clean for piping,
And of a nightingale gone mad with freedom.
Come. I shall weave a bed of reeds
And willow limbs and pale nightflowers.
I shall strip the roses of their petals,
And the white down from the swan's neck.
Come. Night is here. The air is drunk
With wild grape and sweet clover.
And by the sacred fount of Aganippe
Euterpe sings of love. Ah, the woodland creatures,
The doves in pairs, the wild sow and her shoats,
The stag searching the forest for a mate,
Know more of love than you, my callous Phaon.
The young moon is a curved white scimitar
Pierced thru the swooning night.
Sweet Phaon. With Sappho sleep like the stars at
     dawn.
This night was born for love, my Phaon.
Come.

POEM

LITTLE brown boy,
Slim, dark, big-eyed,
Crooning love songs to your banjo
Down at the Lafayette—
Gee, boy, I love the way you hold your head,
High sort of and a bit to one side,
Like a prince, a jazz prince. And I love

Your eyes flashing, and your hands,
And your patent-leathered feet,
And your shoulders jerking the jig-wa.
And I love your teeth flashing,
And the way your hair shines in the spotlight
Like it was the real stuff.
Gee, brown boy, I loves you all over.
I'm glad I'm a jig. I'm glad I can
Understand your dancin' and your
Singin', and feel all the happiness
And joy and don't care in you.
Gee, boy, when you sing, I can close my ears
And hear tom toms just as plain.
Listen to me, will you, what do I know
About tom toms? But I like the word, sort of,
Don't you? It belongs to us.
Gee, boy, I love the way you hold your head,
And the way you sing, and dance,
And everything.
Say, I think you're wonderful. You're
Allright with me,
You are.

FULFILLMENT

To CLIMB a hill that hungers for the sky,
    To dig my hands wrist deep in pregnant earth,
To watch a young bird, veering, learn to fly,
    To give a still, stark poem shining birth.

To hear the rain drool, dimpling, down the drain
   And splash with a wet giggle in the street,
To ramble in the twilight after supper,
   And to count the pretty faces that you meet.

To ride to town on trolleys, crowded, teeming
   With joy and hurry and laughter and push and
      sweat—
Squeezed next a patent-leathered Negro dreaming
   Of a wrinkled river and a minnow net.

To buy a paper from a breathless boy,
   And read of kings and queens in foreign lands,
Hyperbole of romance and adventure,
   All for a penny the color of my hand.

To lean against a strong tree's bosom, sentient
   And hushed before the silent prayer it breathes,
To melt the still snow with my seething body
   And kiss the warm earth tremulous underneath.

Ah, life, to let your stabbing beauty pierce me
   And wound me like we did the studded Christ,
To grapple with you, loving you too fiercely,
   And to die bleeding—consummate with Life.

THE ROAD

Ah, little road all whirry in the breeze,
A leaping clay hill lost among the trees,
The bleeding note of rapture streaming thrush
Caught in a drowsy hush
And stretched out in a single singing line of dusky
    song.
Ah little road, brown as my race is brown,
Your trodden beauty like our trodden pride,
Dust of the dust, they must not bruise you down.
Rise to one brimming golden, spilling cry!

BOTTLED

Upstairs on the third floor
Of the 135th Street library
In Harlem, I saw a little
Bottle of sand, brown sand
Just like the kids make pies
Out of down at the beach.
But the label said: "This
Sand was taken from the Sahara desert."
Imagine that! The Sahara desert!
Some bozo's been all the way to Africa to get some sand.

And yesterday on Seventh Avenue
I saw a darky dressed fit to kill

In yellow gloves and swallow tail coat
And swirling a cane. And everyone
Was laughing at him. Me too,
At first, till I saw his face
When he stopped to hear a
Organ grinder grind out some jazz.
Boy! You should a seen that darky's face!
It just shone. Gee, he was happy!
And he began to dance. No
Charleston or Black Bottom for him.
No sir. He danced just as dignified
And slow. No, not slow either.
Dignified and *proud!* You couldn't
Call it slow, not with all the
Cuttin' up he did. You would a died to see him.

The crowd kept yellin' but he didn't hear,
Just kept on dancin' and twirlin' that cane
And yellin' out loud every once in a while.
I know the crowd thought he was coo-coo.
But say, I was where I could see his face,
And somehow, I could see him dancin' in a jungle,
A real honest-to-cripe jungle, and he wouldn't have on
      them
Trick clothes—those yaller shoes and yaller gloves
And swallow-tail coat. He wouldn't have on nothing.
And he wouldn't be carrying no cane.
He'd be carrying a spear with a sharp fine point
Like the bayonets we had "over there."
And the end of it would be dipped in some kind of

Hoo-doo poison. And he'd be dancin' black and naked
    and gleaming.
And he'd have rings in his ears and on his nose
And bracelets and necklaces of elephants' teeth.
Gee, I bet he'd be beautiful then all right.
No one would laugh at him then, I bet.
Say! That man that took that sand from the Sahara
    desert
And put it in a little bottle on a shelf in the library,
That's what they done to this shine, ain't it? Bottled
    him.
Trick shoes, trick coat, trick cane, trick everything—
    all glass—
But inside—
Gee, that poor shine!

MAGALU

SUMMER comes.
The ziczac hovers
'Round the greedy-mouthed crocodile.
A vulture bears away a foolish jackal.
The flamingo is a dash of pink
Against dark green mangroves,
Her slender legs rivalling her slim neck.
The laughing lake gurgles delicious music in its throat
And lulls to sleep the lazy lizard,
A nebulous being on a sun-scorched rock.

In such a place,
In this pulsing, riotous gasp of color,
I met Magalu, dark as a tree at night,
Eager-lipped, listening to a man with a white collar
And a small black book with a cross on it.
Oh Magalu, come! Take my hand and I will read you
  poetry,
Chromatic words,
Seraphic symphonies,
Fill up your throat with laughter and your heart
  with song.
Do not let him lure you from your laughing waters,
Lulling lakes, lissome winds.
Would you sell the colors of your sunset and the
  fragrance
Of your flowers, and the passionate wonder of your
  forest
For a creed that will not let you dance?

WESLEY CURTWRIGHT

WESLEY CURTWRIGHT was born in Brunswick, Georgia, on November 30, 1910, but he knows as little about Georgia, perhaps, as about any state in the South. Immediately after his father's death in 1913, he began a disjointed tour of the land. He has "broken out in spots" of a dozen states both South and North, attending at intervals various schools. He lives in New York at present and has lived there three years. He is attending Harlem Academy, a small private school. He has contributed to *Opportunity* and *The Messenger*.

THE CLOSE OF DAY

"To MEET and then to part," and that is all,
To slowly turn an album's crusty leaves,
To see the faces and the scenes recall,
Are things that in a lifetime one achieves.

To wander down a broad-arch gallery,
Viewing the scenes from life on either side,
Pressed forward with the force of years to see
But part of every picture when espied.

The big sun in its blue dome keeps its course,
Without a falter moves upon its way.
So human life, returning to its source,
Is overtaken by the close of day.
To dream, and being rudely waked from thought,
Return to peaceful dreaming dearly bought.

LULA LOWE WEEDEN

LULA LOWE WEEDEN was born in Lynchburg, Va., Feb.
4, 1918. Her mother, Mrs. Lula L. Weeden, herself a
poet of ability, writes of this youngest of Negro singers:
"She is a very close observer. Each flower in my garden
she knows. Sometimes she counts each bloom, lingering
over those she likes most.
"Each one of my children is very distinct in her make
up. Lula is quiet, sweet and unselfish, a decided contrast
to the second. This gives each a chance for moral develop-

ment while trying to adjust her little mind to the other. A few nights ago, Iola the second child slapped Mary the baby. Lula said to Iola, 'You are not being a good citizen when you strike back even if Mary did slap you.' An-- other time, Iola was saying what her teacher had said about her. Lula remarked, 'It is not what she says you do, it is what you do do.' Neither statement meant much to Iola.

"I have always mixed my night time stories with ' Home spun ones.' All seem to like them best. I asked Lula since Christmas why she liked my stories. She said because they seemed to be true, and criticized fairy stories.

"I have emphasized racial stories for this reason—I was born on a big farm. There were many employed by my father, also tenants. With these we were not allowed to mingle. On the edge of the farm there was a white school. There was a barrier also. Those little girls with golden locks looked like little angels to me. How I wished to be like them with their shrill voices and laughter. They seemed so happy. I just thought of them as things apart. It took much to get this false conception out of me. They were just God sent. This I have tried not to have my children to fight. Now neither one wishes to be white or dislikes them. To them, they all seem like people.

"Lula does most of her writing at night. It is a priv- ilege to remain a few minutes after the other children to finish something. Some nights she will write several. She mumbles them to herself before she begins to write and then keeps saying the words softly. She will finish this and will draw figures and flowers or people. This she does very well for a child until she says, 'I am going to write something else.' Interruptions don't seem to bother her very much as the little ones are always saying some- thing to make her laugh. I usually attempt to quiet them, but some of her best things are written with many around.

"When she shows them to me, she watches for a favorable expression. I always try to be pleased, but somehow she knows from my face that that was not so good, then remarks, 'I am going to write something else.'

"The amusing part about it all is that she feels as she has begun to write at a mature age, but consoles herself with this statement, 'Stevenson did not begin to write until he was fifteen and wrote very skillful things.'

"Lula is just a little girl and is very talkative if anyone appeals to her and will talk with her. You can't explain anything too minutely for her—whether it is her Sunday school lesson or a star, it matters little."

ME ALONE

As I was going to town,
I saw a King and a Queen.
Such ringing of bells you never heard,
The clerks ran out of the stores;
You know how it was, Me alone.
I was standing as the others were,
"Oh! you little girl," some one said,
"The King wants you,"
I became frightened
Wondering what he had to say,
Me alone.
Here's what he wanted:
He wanted me to ride in his coach,
I felt myself so much riding in a King's coach,
Me alone.

HAVE YOU SEEN IT

HAVE you ever seen the moon
And stars stick together?
Have you ever seen it?
Have you ever seen bad?
Have you ever seen good
And bad stick together?
Have you ever seen it?

ROBIN RED BREAST

LITTLE Robin red breast,
I hear you sing your song.
I would love to have you put it into my little cage,
Into my little mouth.

THE STREAM

IT WAS running down to the great Atlantic.
I called it back to me,
But it slyly looked and said,
"I have not time to waste,"
And just went arunning running on.

THE LITTLE DANDELION

THE dandelion stares
In the yellow sunlight.
How very still it is!
When it is old and grey,
I blow its white hair away,
And leave it with a bald head.

DANCE

DOWN at the hall at midnight sometimes,
You hear them singing rhymes.
These girls are dancing with boys.
They are too big for toys.

INDEX

Absence, 91

Across the dewy lawn she treads, 195

A crust of bread and a corner to sleep in, 5

Advice, 156

A fancy halts my feet at the wayside well, 15

Africa, 123

After All, 191

After the Quarrel, 5

Ah, how poets sing and die, 50

Ah, I know what happiness is, 107

Ah, little road whirry in the breeze, 221

Ah, you are cruel, 47

ALEXANDER, LEWIS, 122

ALLEN, GEORGE LEONARD, 203

All that night I walked alone and wept, 169

All the time they were praying, 208

Although she feeds me bread of bitterness, 83

Always at dusk, the same tearless experience, 37

America, 83

And God stepped out on space, 19

And What Shall You Say? 103

April Day, An, 102

A silence slipping around like death, 46

As I was going to town, 227

A tree is more than a shadow, 170

At the Carnival, 53

Auf Wiedersehen, 189

Baby Cobina, 200

Baker's Boy, The, 58

Band of Gideon, The, 103

Beat the drums of tragedy for me, 148

BENNETT, GWENDOLYN B., 153

Black Madonna, The, 177

Black Man Talks of Reaping, A, 165

Black reapers with the sound of steel on stone, 94

Blight, 170

Boll-weevil's coming, and the winter's cold, 99

BONTEMPS, ARNA, 162

Bottled, 221

Bow down my soul in worship very low, 87

BRAITHWAITE, WILLIAM STANLEY, 31

BROOKS, JONATHAN HENDERSON, 192

Brother, come, 103

Brother to the firefly, 55

BROWN, STERLING A., 129

Brown Baby Cobina, 200

BRUCE, RICHARD, 205

Brushes and paints are all I have, 155

Cavalier, 207

Cemeteries are places for departed souls, 159

Challenge, 138

Chilled into a serenity, 110

Close of Day, The, 225

Close Your Eyes, 171

Come, brother, come. Let's lift it, 97

Confession, 190

Consider me a memory, a dream that passed away, 79

COTTER, JOSEPH S., SR., 10

COTTER, JOSEPH S., JR., 99

Cotton Song, 97
Could I but retrace, 125
Creation, The, 19
Creed, 51
CULLEN, COUNTEE, 179
CUNEY, WARING, 207
CURTWRIGHT, WESLEY, 224

Dance, 229
Dark Brother, The, 124
Day and Night, 129
Day-breakers, The, 171
Dear, when we sit in that high, placid room, 66
Death Bed, The, 208
Death Song, 4
Debt, The, 9
DELANY, CLARISSA SCOTT, 140
Del Cascar, 33
De railroad bridge's a sad song, 147
Deserter, The, 102
Desolate, 88
DICKINSON, BLANCHE TAYLOR, 105
Down at the hall at midnight sometimes, 229
Dream Variation, 149
Dreams of the Dreamer, The, 80
DU BOIS, WILLIAM EDWARD BURGHARDT, 25
DUNBAR, PAUL LAURENCE, 1
Dunbar, 50
Dusk, 46
Dust, 210
Dust, through which proud blood once flowed, 210

Ere Sleep Comes Down to Soothe the Weary Eyes, 2
Evening Song, 94
Exhortation: Summer, 1919, 84
Eyes of My Regret, The, 37

Face, 98
Fantasy, 158
Fantasy in Purple, 148
Father John's bread was made of rye, 31
FAUSET, JESSIE, 64

Flame-flower, Day-torch, Mauna Loa, 52
Flame-Heart, 85
For the Candle Light, 45
For this peculiar tint that paints my house, 92
Four Epitaphs, 186
Four great walls have hemmed me in, 110
Four Walls, 110
Fragment, 70
Frail children of sorrow, dethroned by a hue, 75
From the Dark Tower, 183
From the German of Uhland, 17
Fulfillment, 219
Full moon rising on the waters of my heart, 94

Gay little Girl-of-the-Diving-Tank, 53
Georgia Dusk, 95
Gethsemane, 169
Give over to high things the fervent thought, 182
Glory of the Day Was in Her Face, The, 18
God Give to Men, 172
God give the yellow man, 172
Golgotha Is a Mountain, 173
Go through the gates with closed eyes, 171
Grass Fingers, 38
Greenness, 36
GRIMKÉ, ANGELINA WELD, 35

Hair—silver-gray, like streams of stars, 98
Hatred, 160
Have you ever seen the moon, 228
Have You Seen It, 228
HAYES, DONALD JEFFREY, 188
HAYFORD, GLADYS MAY CASELY, 196
Heart of a Woman, The, 81
He came in silvern armour, trimmed with black, 160
Her eyes? Dark pools of deepest shade, 204

Her love is true I know, 213
He scans the world with calm
  and fearless eyes, 34
He wrote upon his heart, 188
His friends went off and left
  Him dead, 193
Homesick Blues, 147
Homing, 172
Hope, 75
HORNE, FRANK, 111
House in Taos, A, 152
How did it happen that we
  quarreled? 65
HUGHES, LANGSTON, 144
Hushed by the Hands of Sleep, 36

I am so tired and weary, 101
I ask you this, 146
I buried you deeper last night,
  113
I cannot hold my peace, John
  Keats, 184
I do not ask for love, ah! no, 77
I doubt not God is good, 182
I had no thought of violets of
  late, 72
I Have a Friend, 47
I Have a Rendezvous with Life, 180
I have gone back in boyish
  wonderment, 139
I have seen a lovely thing, 170
I have sown beside all waters in
  my day, 165
I have the greatest fun at night,
  58
I kissed a kiss in youth, 31
I know not why or whence he
  came, 102
I know what the caged bird
  feels, alas! 8
I laks yo' kin' of lovin', 134
I long not now, 181
I love you for your brownness,
  157
I love your hands, 44
I return the bitterness, 124
I said, in drunken pride of youth
  and you, 138
I sailed in my dreams to the
  Land of Night, 158

I see in your eyes, 178
I shall come this way again, 189
I shall hate you, 160
I shall make a song like your
  hair, 155
I should like to creep, 42
I Sit and Sew, 73
I that had found the way so
  smooth, 70
I Think I See Him There, 210
I think that man hath, 204
I thought I saw an angel flying
  low, 166
I Too, 145
*I Want to Die While You Love
  Me,* 78
I Weep, 45
I went to court last night, 63
If I have run my course and
  seek the pearls, 64
If my garden oak spares one
  bare ledge, 51
I'm folding up my little dreams,
  79
Incident, 187
Innocence, 51
Inscription, 188
Interim, 142
In wintertime I have such fun,
  59
Is Life itself but many ways of
  thought, 48
It crawled away 'neath my feet,
  109
It is fitting that you be here, 112
It was running down to the great
  Atlantic, 228
I've known rivers, 149

Japanese Hokku, 127
Jericho is on the inside, 106
JOHNSON, FENTON, 61
JOHNSON, GEORGIA DOUGLAS, 74
JOHNSON, HELENE, 215
JOHNSON, JAMES WELDON, 15
Joy, 140
Joy shakes me like the wind that
  lifts a sail, 140
Jungle Taste, 214

Lady, my lady, come from out the garden, 136
Lancelot, 169
Last Quarter Moon of the Dying Year, The, 195
La Vie C'est La Vie, 69
Lay me down beneaf de willers in de grass, 4
Lemme be wid Casey Jones, 130
Length of Moon, 168
Lethe, 77
Let me learn now where Beauty is, 48
Letters Found Near a Suicide, 114
Life, 5
Life-Long, Poor Browning, 49
Lines to a Nasturtium, 52
Lines Written at the Grave of Alexander Dumas, 159
Litany of Atlanta, A, 26
Little black boy, 120
Little brown boy, 218
Little Dandelion, The, 229
Little Robin red breast, 228
Little Son, 76
"Lo, I am black but I am comely too," 124
Lolotte, who attires my hair, 67
Long Gone, 134
Long have I beat with timid hands, 76

Magalu, 223
Marathon Runner, The, 64
Mask, The, 143
MATHEUS, JOHN FREDERICK, 60
Maumee Ruth, 133
McCALL, JAMES EDWARD, 33
McKAY, CLAUDE, 81
Me Alone, 227
Men never know, 212
Might as well bury her, 133
Mona Lisa, A, 42
Morning Light, 55
Mother to Son, 151
My City, 25
My heart that was so passionless, 70
My House, 92
My Little Dreams, 79

My little stone, 114
My spirit is a pestilential city, 88
My window opens out into the trees, 141

Nativity, 197
Negro Speaks of Rivers, The, 149
Negro Woman, 122
Neighbors, 47
NELSON, ALICE DUNBAR, 71
New Negro, The, 34
NEWSOME, MARY EFFIE LEE, 55
Nigger, 120
Night, 189
Night like purple flakes of snow, 189
Noblesse Oblige, 67
Nocturne, 190
Nocturne at Bethesda, 166
No Images, 212
Northboun', 201
Not as the white nations, 177
Not to dance with her, 209
November Cotton Flower, 99

O apple blossoms, 127
O brothers mine, take care! Take care! 22
October XXIX, 1795, 32
O' de wurl' ain't flat, 201
Odyssey of Big Boy, 130
Oh, the blue, blue bloom, 56
Old Black Men, 77
Once more, listening to the wind and rain, 163
Once riding in old Baltimore, 187
On Seeing Two Brown Boys in a Catholic Church, 112
On such a day as this I think, 102
On summer afternoons I sit, 69
On the dusty earth-drum, 100
O Silent God, Thou whose voice afar, 26
Out in the sky the great clouds are massing, 7
Out of the tense awed darkness, 198
O you would clothe me in silken frocks, 87

Paean, 195
Pansy, 56
Paradox, 43
Poem, 107
Poem, 150
Poem, 218
Portrait, 204
Pour O pour that parting soul in song, 96
Prayer, 146
Protest, 181
Proving, 77
Puck Goes to Court, 63
Puppet Player, The, 46

Quatrains, 155
Questing, 48
Quilt, The, 58
Quoits, 59

Radical, The, 212
Rain Music, 100
Rainy Season Love Song, 198
Reapers, 94
Recessional, 79
Rencontre, 70
Requiem, 61
Resurrection, The, 193
Return, 139
Return, The, 70
Return, The, 163
Revelation, 107
RICE, ALBERT, 176
Road, The, 221
Robin Red Breast, 228
Russian Cathedral, 87
Rye Bread, 31

Salutamus, 138
Sassafras Tea, 56
Scintilla, 31
Secret, 155
Service, 75
Serving Girl, The, 200
Shadow, 206
She does not know, 212
She kneeled before me begging, 190
She tripped and fell against a star, 51

She walked along the crowded street, 107
She wears, my beloved, a rose upon her head, 61
Ships That Pass in the Night, 7
Silhouette on the face of the moon, 206
SILVERA, EDWARD S., 213
Sky Pictures, 57
Slay fowl and beast; pluck clean the vine, 207
Snow in October, 71
So detached and cool she is, 143
Softly blow lightly, 190
Solace, 141
Some things are very dear to me, 161
Sometimes a right white mountain, 57
Sometimes it seems as though some puppet player, 46
So much have I forgotten in ten years, 85
Song for a Dark Girl, 147
Song of the Son, 96
Sonnet, 72
Sonnet, 160
Sonnet, 161
Sonnet to a Negro in Harlem, 217
South Street, 214
So we, who've supped the self-same cup, 5
SPENCER, ANNE, 47
Stream, The, 228
Substitution, 48
Suicide's Note, 151
Summer comes, 223
Summer Matures, 217
Suppliant, The, 76
Supplication, 101
Surrender, 38
Sweet timber land, 172
Sympathy, 8

Tanka, 125
Tell me is there anything lovelier, 36
Tenebris, 40
That Hill, 109

The baker's boy delivers loaves, 58

The band of Gideon roam the sky, 103

The bitterness of days like these we know, 138

The breath of life imbued those few dim days, 70

The calabash wherein she served my food, 200

The calm, 151

The dandelion stares, 229

The day is a Negro, 129

The fruit of the orchard is over-ripe, Elaine, 169

The heart of a woman goes forth with the dawn, 81

The hills are wroth; the stones have scored, 165

The night is beautiful, 150

The night was made for rest and sleep, 142

Then the golden hour, 168

There is a coarseness, 214

There is a tree, by day, 40

There was a man, 11

The sass'fras tea is red and clear, 56

The sky hangs heavy tonight, 122

The sky, lazily disdaining to pursue, 95

The sky was blue, so blue that day, 45

The very acme of my woe, 76

They have dreamed as young men dream, 77

This is the debt I pay, 9

This lovely flower fell to seed, 186

Thou art not dead, although the spoiler's hand, 123

Three students once tarried over the Rhine, 17

Through the pregnant universe, 84

Thunder of the Rain God, 152

Time sitting on the throne of Memory, 32

'Tis queer, it is, the ways to men, 39

To a Certain Lady, in Her Garden, 136

To a Certain Woman, 178

To a Dark Girl, 157

To an Icicle, 110

To a Persistent Phantom, 113

To a Young Girl Leaving the Hill Country, 165

To climb a hill that hungers for the sky, 219

Today I saw a thing of arresting poignant beauty, 71

To fling my arms wide, 149

To John Keats, Poet, at Spring-time, 184

To Lovers of Earth: Fair Warning, 182

"To meet and then to part," 225

To Melody, 204

TOOMER, JEAN, 93

Touché, 66

Touch me, touch me, 38

Tragedy of Pete, The, 11

Transformation, 124

Tree Design, A, 170

Triviality, A, 209

True Love, 213

Twin stars through my purpling pane, 46

Upstairs on the third floor, 221

Walls of Jericho, The, 106

Way down South in Dixie, 147

Way-side Well, The, 15

Ways o' Men, The, 39

We are not come to wage a strife, 171

We ask for peace. We, at the bound, 38

WEEDEN, LULA LOWE, 225

Well, son, I'll tell you, 151

Were you a leper bathed in wounds, 77

We shall not always plant while others reap, 183

We Wear the Mask, 8

What Do I Care for Morning, 216

What Need Have I for Memory?
80
What! Roses growing in the
meadow, 59
When face to face we stand, 43
When first you sang a song to
me, 157
When I am Dead, 80
When I come down to sleep
death's endless night, 25
When I Die, 62
*When the Green Lies Over the
Earth,* 41
When we count out our gold at
the end of the day, 75

White Witch, The, 22
Wild Goat, The, 87
Wild Roses, 59
WILLIAMS, LUCY ARIEL, 201
Winter Twilight, A, 46
Within a native hut, 197
Words! Words! 65

Yet Do I Marvel, 182
You are disdainful and magnifi-
cent, 217
Your Hands, 44
Your Songs, 157
Your words dropped into my
heart, 91
You were a sophist, 156